THE WORD AS REVELATION
NAMES OF GODS

The Word as Revelation Names of Gods

RAM SWARUP

FOREWORD BY
David Frawley
(Vamadeva Shastri)

VOICE OF INDIA
New Delhi

First Published: 1980
First Reprint: 2001
Reprint, 2024

ISBN 81-85990-68-9

Published by Voice of India, 2/18, Ansari Road, New Delhi – 110 002
and printed at Replika Press Pvt. Ltd.

Contents

Transliteration

Devanāgarī	*Roman*	*sounds like*		
Vowels				
अ	a	u	in	sun
आ	ā	a	”	far
इ	i	i	”	fill
ई	ī	ee	”	seed
उ	u	oo	”	book
ऊ	ū	oo	”	moon
ऋ	ṛ	r	”	verily
ॠ	ṝ	r	”	marine
ऌ	lṛ	lr	”	chivalry
ए	e	a	”	ray
ऐ	ai	e	”	red
ओ	o	o	”	go
औ	au	a	”	all
अं	ṃ	(Anusvāra)		
:	ḥ	(Visarga)		
Consonants				
gutturals				
क्	k	k	in	king
ख्	kh*	kh	”	sinkhole
ग्	g	g	”	good
घ्	gh*	gh	”	doghouse
ङ्	ṅ+	n	”	king
palatals				
च्	c	ch	in	church
छ्	ch*	chh	”	witch hunt
ज्	j	j	”	jar
झ्	jh*	g(e)h	”	bridgehead
ञ्	ñ+	n	”	range

Devanāgarī	*Roman*	*sounds like*		
Cerebrals				
ट्	ṭ	t	in	true
ठ्	ṭh*	th	"	hothouse
ड्	ḍ	d	"	day
ढ्	ḍh*	dh	"	red-haired
ण्	ṇ			aspirate nasal
Dentals				
त्	t	soft	t	as in French
थ्	th	th	"	truth
द्	d	th	"	they
ध्	dh*	dh	"	adhere
न्	n⁺	n	"	now
Labials				
प्	p	p	in	pen
फ्	ph*	ph	"	uphill
ब्	b	b	"	book
भ्	bh*	bh	"	abhor
म्	m	m	"	moon
Semi-Vowels				
य्	y	y	in	yellow
र्	r	r	"	rain
ल्	l	l	"	lamp
व्	v	w	"	war
Sibilants				
श्	ś⁺	sh	in	ship
ष्	ṣ⁺	sh	"	shun
स्	s⁺	s	"	sun
Aspirate				
ह	h	h	in	high

*English does not have the equivalents of Sanskrit aspirate mutes. So the sounds given for kh, gh, ch, jh, ṭh, ḍh, ph, bh are approximations.

⁺The difference between nasal sounds like ṅ, ñ, ṇ, n is non-significant in English. Even in Hindi, they have a tendency to run into one single sound of n. Similarly, the distinction between the two sibilants ś and ṣ is on the wane.

Foreword

"Mortals, of thou the Immortal, we meditate upon your many names." Vatsa Kāṇva, Rigveda VIII.11.5.

In *The Word as Revelation: Names of Gods*, Ram Swarup explores the core issues of religion, culture and spirituality for all humanity. He examines speech, language and communication starting from an ordinary level leading to the human attempt to communicate with the Divine and the Infinite. His book causes the reader to create a new relationship with language and look at words with careful consideration, if not deep contemplation. Our words carry power and motivation, not simply their meaning as found in the dictionary. They influence others deeply whether we intend them to or not, and in ways that go beyond what words literally or figuratively indicate. Words shape our minds and become the raw material out of which we create our culture and ourselves.

Following Upanishadic thought one could say that speech is the essence of the human being. Speaking is our main motor activity in life and our most characteristic expression as a species. Yet speech is a power that we have not often used wisely or shaped consciously. Only rare enlightened beings have discovered the real power of the word and used it as a liberating force for the spirit. For most of us and for our culture in general words are mainly propaganda tools and transmit various prejudices and stereotypes. They do not communicate and unite but separate and isolate into warring camps.

Our words are psychic containers that hold certain memories and experiences, not only our own but of our entire society. Each word has a history and carries the weight of thought and emotion of those who have used it over time. Words grow and develop in positive or negative ways, just as our culture can evolve or decline spiritually or materially. Indeed words are like Gods or cosmic powers in their own right. They shape us from on high and can inspire us to transcend our human limitations. However, words can also function like demons and stir up our baser inclinations. Words can be tools of wonderful creation or wicked weapons of corruption and destruction. Unless we use them consciously they can cause unforeseen difficulties that we may not be able to control. If we do use them consciously, they can work wonders and transform the heart, mind and soul.

Revelation: A Blessing or a Curse?

Ram Swarup's study focuses on the spiritual dimension of language in which the word is the vehicle of a higher perception. This is what he means by revelation—a revealing of the higher truth directly to the receptive human mind. However, he also examines the entire issue of revelation in various traditions East and West.

The different scriptures of the world speak of 'revelation' or the existence of a Divine Word beyond our mere human speech. They know of an Eternal Word beyond our transient human mutterings. They recognize a higher form of knowledge revealed through this Divine Word—which occurs in a transcendent state of consciousness—a Supreme Truth that affords sure guidance how to live rightly and shows the way to immortality.

All cultures from the most ancient times have teachings about the Divine Word, the Names of God, or Names of Gods and Goddesses. All ancient cultures have their great sages, seers, prophets and rishis who proclaimed this Divine Word to a particular people or culture. Often, as in the case of ancient India, these sages were the original founders of the civilization of the region.

Certainly such revelations are one of the greatest legacies of humanity and the key to much of culture even today. All over the world ancient and medieval scriptures remain the most commonly read, spoken and chanted books. They inspire the greatest amount of human behavior in the entire spectrum from loving kindness to vicious terrorism.

Unfortunately, several so-called scriptures or their interpreters proclaim their revelation in a parochial manner. They say that they alone have the Word of God and no one else. They identify the Supreme and Eternal Word of God with a particular historical document that is really the product of a few human beings and not the Divine Word at all (which is not entirely expressible in this material world anyway). They condemn those outside their particular revelation to damnation or at least to everlasting inferiority. For this reason the term 'revelation' today inspires as much fear as faith and rightly so.

These exclusive religious traditions grant their founders a unique ability to transmit revelation that other human beings are barred from achieving. Their prophets or Son of God alone are given the ability to mediate between God and humanity and communicate God's wishes to the world, without which the ordinary mortal is lost. In these traditions revelation is a unique event that future generations can only read, imitate and try to follow but cannot themselves directly experience. For other traditions—particularly those beyond the pale of Western monotheism and its characteristic rigidity—revelation and spiritual realization are the potential and ultimate goal of all human beings. Teachers may be necessary but a special prophethood or saviorhood is a distortion, if not an impediment.

This arrogation of revelation occurs in the Christian tradition that turn the Bible—which is essentially the religious document of the Jewish people—into an eternal truth for all humanity, the supreme and final scripture. It similarly occurs in Islam, which turns the Koran—the revelation of Mohammed, a single person—into a lasting, final and supreme revelation for all humanity. For such traditions the Divine Word belongs to certain historical leaders who serve as its intermediaries for the rest of humanity, who must rely on their interpretations and follow their injunctions. The Divine Word is not a human birthright but a special dispensation to the chosen one who in turn passes it on to the rest of humanity from on high. Such a Divine messenger not surprisingly becomes more important than the Divine itself. People can only know what God wants of them through the savior or messenger and his prescriptions. Anything else is heretical. People are dependent upon the words of the messenger and fail to develop their own internal connection to the Divine. They remain trapped in the shadow of his personality and the events of his particular life.

Revelation of truth and communion with the Divine Word—Ram Swarup emphasizes—is not the possession of certain monotheistic religions but is a characteristic of religion and spirituality as a whole. It is not something owned by a prophet, book or church but is a matter of individual communion with Divinity that rests upon a certain state of mind and specific spiritual practices. Those who speak of revelation as a mere book have not experienced the revelation of truth at all. This requires a higher state of consciousness in which one goes beyond external names, forms and institutions.

Traditions that emphasize spiritual and mystical experience over any church—such as both Pagan and Eastern Dharmic traditions—abound in revelation as a higher form of perception. They have well-defined yogic and mystical practices so that anyone can arrive at union with the Divine. The Indic tradition recognizes higher forms of seeing and hearing (*drishṭi* and *śruti*) that reflect this. Great Pagan savants like Apollonius or Plotinus had their revelations as glorious as any Biblical vision. Pagan traditions like the Druids have had their sacred languages and holy books as extensive as the Bible.

Unfortunately, monotheistic traditions try to own revelation and reduce it to their books and prophets alone. They deny any direct knowledge of the Divine outside their tradition. They even deny their members any direct revelation of their own and make them go through the intermediary of the book or prophet. Such monotheistic revelations are limited, reduced to a person or historical event, and fail to open up their followers to the inner truth of consciousness. Their believers often take them literally, which results in intolerance and the need to convert others to a belief. This expropriation of revelation becomes a good justification for condemning others as unholy. It is also the end of any real revelation for those who are involved in it.

Ram Swarup points out the dangers inherent in arrogating the Word of God. Speaking in the name of God contains a great potential for deception, not only of others but also of oneself. It is gratifying to think that God speaks to us or through us. It can be the greatest glorification possible of the ego. We note how fundamentalist preachers in America proclaim 'God says' when they are just projecting their own prejudices. Or they say that 'God says in the Bible' as if it were the last word on anything, ignoring the fact that the Bible is hardly the Word of God and has many layers and opinions both high and low that can be interpreted in various ways. This idea of exclusive revelation—which leads to the need to bring the world under one religious banner—has caused untold confusion and misery in this world. It is not true revelation but rather a darkening of the light.

As Ram Swarup explains, such religious beliefs reflect an ego state of consciousness. They may have a connection with the Divine but it is distorted—filtered by an impure or immature mind. They want to possess the truth as if it were a material object and turn it into an institution. Their literalism is nothing but spiritual materialism. Their religion becomes more a political practice of conversion than any internal meditation, whose importance they may not even know.

Such credal beliefs are content with what is at best second-hand knowledge. They are not seeking a higher consciousness for humanity but merely imposing a label on people, as if that would somehow magically make everyone holy. Along with their belief in revelation comes every sort of superstition including eternal heaven and hell and the impending end of the world. While it would be easy to dismiss such beliefs as merely childish, Ram Swarup shows that they carry a tremendous psychic force, energized by a one-sided emotion that can easily become destructive. Certainly their effect upon humanity has been enormous and their emotional force has often overwhelmed more intelligent peoples and cultures. This is because they mix spiritual truth and ego together, which is a very dangerous and volatile combination. The problem is that nectar mixed with poison becomes poison.

The Divine Word in Indic Traditions

To truly approach the Divine Word first requires a purification of our own minds and hearts. This is an internal broadening of our nature in which we cease to identify ourselves with a mere body or even with a single culture. It is not a matter of accepting a prophet, savior or scripture, however great, but of genuine self-knowledge. This, however, is much more difficult to do than loudly proclaiming a belief to a spiritually untrained and unprepared audience. It requires real meditation, critical introspection and self-examination on an individual level.

From the standpoint of Indic or Dharmic traditions the Divine Word or the Word of God can never be identified with any single book or with the utterance of any particular prophet, however great. It is a state of consciousness, not a written text that must be subject to misinterpretation. It is the word of truth inscribed into the heart that transcends all formulations. To discover that Divine Word requires individual *sādhanā* or spiritual practice. It cannot come from another, from the outside, from a book, though such things can help catalyze its internal manifestation if they are approached with humility and understanding.

The Vedas, the oldest spiritual teaching and root revelation of the Indic tradition, reflect the mantras of various sages who were able to reach a state of cosmic consciousness in which they could commune directly with the Divine Word. They do not rest upon any particular personality. Their purpose is not to promote a belief but to connect us with Dharma or cosmic law, ultimately to connect us with our own individual nature or *svadharma* and a realization of the Divine Self, the Atman within.

To truly liberate our consciousness we must open up to the full force and manifestation of the Divine Word that transcends all external forms, persons and revelations. That is the real challenge of spirituality, not merely accepting and blindly following a particular text. In fact, the Divine Word itself has a level of meaning that transcends all human language. It is a metalanguage of sound, symbol, energy and consciousness that unfolds many dimensions of meaning and power and cannot be circumscribed into the box of belief or the coffins of dogma. It is mantra, not philosophy, theology or debate, much less propaganda, injunctions or prescriptions of rewards and punishments.

The Issue of Language

Of course we have little use for the Divine Word today. Ours is the age of advertising and political slogans, which extends to religion. Our scriptures are old and dead books that we take literally in order to freeze our minds so that we don't have to think seriously about life. We are content with propaganda, marketing and stereotypes, none of which can open up the real power of revelation or direct insight that most of us cannot even imagine anyway. Compared to the ancient languages our modern tongues suffer from a profound spiritual poverty. Our words are like sand. They cannot be compared to the nectar of the ancient sages. We lack the very words to express higher truths. The words we do have, like the word 'God' itself, more easily perpetuate prejudices than convey anything transcendent.

This issue of the Divine Word takes us to the issue of language itself. Language contains the history of a culture. The development of its words shows the development of the civilization. Each word in a language is like a *saṃskāra* for the culture. It holds the memory and the tendencies of the culture and carries them on to future generations. It can teach us a lot if we are receptive to what it really indicates. Look at how little of the sacred remains in our speech. No wonder there is so little meaning or depth in our lives.

Actually all language should be an effort to express the Divine

Word. It should be a means of ennobling ourselves and reaching out to the greater universe of consciousness. In the Hindu view speech itself is the Goddess Sarasvati and should be honored as such. We should let Sarasvati speak through us, rather than seeking to impose our own voice upon the world. Language today, however, has little Sarasvati in it. Rather, it is an Asuric formation to control and manipulate that takes shape as the mass media and its growing violence. Unless we stop this process and respiritualize the world through the Divine Word, our culture must eventually collapse.

The Sanskrit Language

Ram Swarup's study revolves around various key Sanskrit terms. Sanskrit itself is a Divine language, the reputed language of the Gods. Every word, in fact every syllable of it, naturally becomes a Divine Name. The Vedas themselves, the origin of the Sanskrit language, are powerhouses of Divine Names. Vedic language is a sophisticated vehicle for invoking the Divine, not only in general but also relative to specific needs and issues of life, spiritual and mundane. The energy hidden in the Vedic language can transform our entire consciousness, both individually and collectively, if we open up to it and practice it regularly. This is how the ancient enlightened Vedic culture was created and sustained.

The worship of the name, *nāma*, occurs everywhere in the Indic tradition from the Rigveda itself. It characterizes the entire Hindu religion. Each God or Goddess is a Name of the Supreme Divine in one aspect or angle of approach. Each great God or Goddess like Shiva, Vishnu or Devi has his or her own thousand Names that encompass all of reality, personal and impersonal, formed and formless. Meditation on the Divine Names and Mantras is one of the main Vedic paths. It is the basis of Bhaktiyoga, the yoga of devotion. Each Name reflects an aspect of Divine or a relationship with the Divine for us to emulate in our hearts.

Ram Swarup shows how such an honoring of the Divine Names extended from the Vedic era to later Hinduism. He shows how it is reflected in the other religions of the world, including in the Pagan traditions that have been denigrated as unholy and devoid of revelation. The religions that claim to own God or restrict divinity to one formulation are not the real bearers of the sacred, but conceal the mischief of the anti-gods whose role is to usurp and distort the powers of the Gods. Many Gods and Goddesses reflect the richness of the Divine Name that is the basis of all qualities and all functions in the universe. They reflect an infinite unity, not a divided multiplicity. Each Divine Name has its personality and power that can be envisioned in the form of a particular deity, which in turn becomes a doorway to the Infinite.

Pagan Traditions

Pagan traditions honor many Names and Forms of God, just like Hinduism, the world's oldest and largest Pagan tradition. They abound in revelation as a living reality, not merely as an old book. There is more of the Divine Word in their teachings than most of what we call monotheism. They see the Word of God in the hills, the vales, the rivers and the clouds. They show us how the book of Nature is itself the manifestation of the Divine. Their various Gods and Goddesses are various Divine Names, not separate entities, just as the Gods and Goddesses of Hinduism.

Pagan traditions, including the Native American, are well aware of a single Great Spirit manifesting through these many Names and Forms. But that Great Spirit or Brahman is a cosmic truth and consciousness, not an imperialistic Creator, intolerant, jealous and seeking to impose his will on all. This vision of the Great Spirit echoes the Upanishadic view that the Purusha or conscious being is everywhere in Nature.

Of course we must remember that the word 'pagan' itself is a pejorative term, a slur of denigration like heathen or kafir. Pagan originally referred to 'peasant', as the countryside people of the Roman Empire held on to the old religions longer than their urban counterparts that were more under the rule of the state. Pagan eventually came to mean non-Biblical beliefs of all types, particularly those that the Biblical traditions opposed and eradicated, including the glorious spiritual and occult traditions of Egypt and Babylonia.

The word 'pagan' is part of a whole set of negative religious terms including 'polytheist' and 'idolater' that include some of the most negative appellations found in human language. These are part of a kind of language of demonizing—for discrediting those of other religious backgrounds as unholy—including rejecting their revelations as not only wrong but evil. These terms are like racial slurs such as nigger, which were used to impose racism and to promote the oppression of one race by another. They similarly impose religious exclusivism and promote the oppression of one religion by another.

To really approach the Divine Word we must set such negative terms aside and embrace the Divine Word in all of its forms. When some absolute evil, eternal hell or Satan is placed in opposition to the Divine Word, it turns the Divine Word into intolerance. The true Divine Word is not caught in such duality. It overcomes darkness with light and shows a hidden Divine light even behind suffering and ignorance. The Pagan traditions show the Divine presence in all aspects of life, embracing duality and multiplicity in a creative and a transcendent unity. The monotheistic rejection of their teachings is a rejection of a higher truth and more many-sided understanding.

Ram Swarup sets forth a clarion call to non-Biblical (Pagan) and Native traditions to revive their ancient Gods and Goddesses. He encourages them to return to their ancient ways, to restore a broader, pluralistic approach to Divinity and reformulate it anew in the modern world. He requests them to study and connect with the Hindu tradition as an aid and ally in this process.

This awakening of Pagan and Native traditions is a necessary part of humanity reawakening to its greater spiritual heritage—the legacy of the ancient seers within us—which is not promoting a single belief but opening many paths to Self-realization. The ancient Gods and Goddesses contain our older and deeper spiritual impulses that we need to energize once more today in order to really grow in consciousness and integrate as a species.

Once more invoking their Names is a means of this regeneration. The Gods and Goddesses represent our higher Selves that have been frozen by beliefs and institutions and must once more be set free to restore our spiritual vitality in life.

Ram Swarup also promotes a new scholarship that looks at these older traditions in a spiritual light and honors their critiques of the religions that have denigrated them. We find that these diverse traditions have more spiritual wisdom and grant a deeper spiritual experience to their members than the more monotone religions that displaced them and still seek to eradicate them. We have been taught to look at Pagan and Native traditions according to the jaded views of an exclusive monotheism. We now need to look at monotheism from the viewpoint of these more mystical traditions that it has opposed. Once we do this we find that monotheism is not the supreme truth it has been portrayed to be, but a lesser truth that we must transcend.

We see the ancient and Eastern Gods and Goddesses awakening today as part of the expanding consciousness of the dawning planetary age. The Earth itself is the main Goddess that we must honor again. It is time for humanity to embrace all of its revelations, all of its Gods and Goddesses. This requires going beyond the limitations of monotheism, which is only one aspect of the human religious experience. It requires that we contact our true Self of which the entire universe is a manifestation. Monotheism, polytheism, pantheism, dualism and monism are but facets of the same Reality that cannot be limited by an ideology or a belief.

Sound and Consciousness

According to yogic philosophy, sound is the sensory quality that belongs to the element of ether (*ākāśa*). Ether is the subtlest of the elements and the origin of all of them, the great matrix or prima materia. Sound, through creating and controlling ether or space, creates and sustains the entire universe. All that we see is a manifestation of vibration, sound or the cosmic word. Yet there is not only the material space but also the space of the mind. This has its own kind of sound, which is thought vibration. The mind itself is like space, which is the basis of perception. When the mind has space we are happy and wise. When the mind is constricted we are disturbed and biased.

Beyond the mind-space is the space of consciousness, an infinite expanse in which there is everlasting peace, bliss and love. This space of consciousness (*cid-ākāśa*) is reflected in the Divine Names, which are the truth-vibrations that it carries. The Divine Word is the inherent self-expressive power of pure consciousness. This Divine Word in the space of pure consciousness is what creates, sustains and dissolves the universe.

The Word as I am

The true Divine Word is of the nature of I am (*aham*). It is the supreme Self, Paramātman, in its self-articulation. This I am is the basis of consciousness. The Divine I am or Paramātman dwells in the hearts of all beings as their own soul and self, Jīvātman. This I am (Atman) that is the vibration of consciousness is also Brahman or the Absolute. It is of the nature of infinite expansion (*brihaṃaṇa*). Throughout the universe the I am is ever proclaiming itself in various worlds and creatures, ever unfolding its unlimited being in ever-changing ways.

In the Vedantic view there is only one valid relationship that we have, not only with the Divine but with all beings. It is not "I and thou". It is certainly not "I and you." It is "I and I", the Self to the Self. This is also the inner meaning of the great mantra OM. The Divine Name is a relationship of I to I or Self to Self in which we mere humans can work with the Gods.

This Divine Word is also energy. Space through sound creates Prāṇa, which is the movement of life. Through its pranic force the Divine Word energizes and enlivens all things. To the extent that we partake of it we become filled not only with wisdom but also with vitality. This Divine Word is not simply the fiat or fatwa of a monotheistic Father God, judging all creatures from his throne above. It is the creative utterance and formation of Dharma. It is the very foundation of cosmic law and sustains the order of karma and rebirth in the universe. This Divine Word is not only the basis of the Creator but of the many Gods and Goddesses that are the different names, forms and functions of the Creator in the diverse aspects of creation.

The Divine Word is not simply male; in fact it is primarily feminine. In the Vedic view speech or the word is feminine, is the very form of the Goddess or Divine Mother. The letters of the Sanskrit alphabet are the great mothers that create the world. The Word forms, nourishes and protects us like a mother. Actually all names belong to the Divine, as do all forms. There is only One Being and Consciousness behind the diversity of names and forms in the entire universe. It embraces all things and excludes only partiality.

Ram Swarup

In his approach to the Vedas, Ram Swarup follows in the footsteps of great modern Vedic interpreters like Sri Aurobindo and Swami Dayananda of the Arya Samaj. Dayananda felt that all the names of the Vedic Gods were simply different names of the One Truth or Divine Reality. Sri Aurobindo more clearly delineated how each name relates to a different aspect of Divinity and a different path to wholeness as part of the yogic quest. Ram Swarup develops this vision yet further.

The Word as Revelation is probably Ram Swarup's most mystical book. It shows the spiritual root of his thinking that had a firm basis in the Divine Word. His deep mind and vast interests also compelled him to write on political, social and historical issues—not for his own benefit, as he could clearly see the truth of such matters—but for others who had the intellectual potential but lacked the teachings to help them see the truth. Yet Ram Swarup remained primarily a seer, philosopher and poet and was not himself tainted or disturbed by such controversies. So one could say that this is perhaps the core book of his inspiration. It is a good companion to his *Meditations: Yogas, Gods, Religions*. It also interfaces well with his studies of Christianity and Islam and helps us understand his critique of them.

The Power of the Name

Names have many mysterious powers. They link us with the object, being or person that they signify, connecting us telepathically to its energy and its qualities. They allow us to call, invoke or manifest it in our own lives. We must be careful in the names we choose and the names we invoke. They can magnify not only the spiritual power of *sattvaguṇa* but also the material powers of *rajas* and *tamas* depending on their nature. By invoking Divine Names we also call those Divine qualities and powers to manifest within us. We awaken our own *sattva*. Yet if we invoke the Divine out of lower motives of *rajas* and *tamas*—to conquer, control, dominate others or impose our desires and beliefs upon them—what we are doing will be more black magic or psychic violence than anything truly spiritual.

Let us therefore endeavor to contact these Divine Names and work with them in our own lives. Let us not merely repeat their sounds but etch their meanings deep within our hearts, which requires determined meditation upon them. That is the best way to honor great teachings like the Vedas and to honor great teachers like Ram Swarup who are trying to help us contact that Divine Word directly. Let that Divine Utterance arise within us in which our personal limitations are dissolved and in which the universal truth can again manifest in this material world!

Santa Fe, New Mexico, USA
Kārtika Pūrṇimā
November 11, 2000

DAVID FRAWLEY
(Vamadeva Shastri)

Preface

The present volume was unintended. It was not conceived in the form it has assumed.

There are two opposing views about language, both advanced by distinguished thinkers. One view holds that a language is external to objects and thoughts; the other view regards it as fundamental to them. Some say that in the beginning was the word and the word was with God and the word was God; others preach that words are God-eclipsing and soul-veiling; and yet some others hold that words in any role other than that of physical referents are deceptive and even the words God and Soul are a linguistic trick. In what sense or senses are these views true? Can they be reconciled?

One reason for taking up these questions was that we wanted to make for ourselves some sense out of the Vedas, the oldest Hindu scriptures and indeed the oldest extant literature of the Aryan race. We wondered if an archaic glossary concealed their obscure meanings; or if there was a code that needed decoding for their proper understanding or if there was a certain number of key-words which had to be properly understood before the Vedas yielded the meanings they held.

These and other related questions and interests led us to reflection on language itself. And hence the present study.

But though the book started as an inquiry into language, it soon passed into questions of psychology, philosophy, theology, yoga, and meditation. This turn was inevitable considering the interest with which we started. We also believe that any worthwhile inquiry into linguistics must merge into an inquiry into the nature of Reality. The roots of a language go deep into the soil of man's being. So, we hope that readers will see that there is nothing forced about this approach; that it is a natural, beautiful and true coming together of things which are inevitably related; and that the fusion is no confusion.

How are things named and how do names acquire their larger meanings? In a sense, these questions are central to any inquiry into the phenomenon of language; but a language could also be studied in its more external though quite important and legitimate aspects: acoustic, phonetic, neural, philological, etymological, etc. These are precisely the aspects on which the present-day studies of linguistics try to concentrate with considerably happy results. These studies have yielded nothing new but they have confirmed some old insights. They have not been able to enter the citadel but their peripheral reconnoitering is not without its use and interest. The present study makes use of their labour but it also has its own approach and temper and develops the subject in its own way. It treats the subject psychologically, and even meta-psychologically, that is, in terms of deeper levels of consciousness accessible only to yogic meditation, and belonging to a different discipline and quest of life. It has followed an analytical approach in order to build up a larger synthesis.

If we keep all this in view, it should help to answer some possible objections which were in fact made by some friends. They thought that the book discussed only names when a language is more than names. It is, for example, also parts of speech, syntax, grammar. The argument is valid. But, as we have said, the book is not about language as such; nor does it study it in the spirit of present-day sciences of linguistics; on the contrary, it is about names and their meanings, particularly the higher ones. Therefore, naturally, the treatment of the subject is lexical, dealing with the vocabulary of a language as distinguished from its grammar and construction.

Another objection was that, in tracing the etymologies of various words, we have stopped short at old Sanskrit forms whereas we should have gone back to Indo-European roots. Are we suggesting that Sanskrit is the mother language and modern European languages are derived from it?

To this objection our answer is that the purpose of this study is not etymology as such; but etymology has been used to the extent it shows that words have life, vivacity, suggestions, signification, resilience, adaptation. They live, grow, symbolize, associate with each other like living things. For this purpose the old Sanskrit forms will do as well as the Indo-European roots. But the former have one advantage over the latter: they have a living tradition behind them.

Webster's Seventh New Collegiate Dictionary defines Etymology as the history of a linguistic form (as a word) shown by tracing its development since its *earliest recorded occurrence* in the language where it is found, by tracing its transmission from one language to another, by analyzing it into its component parts, by identifying its cognates in other languages, or by tracing it and its cognates to a common ancestral form in an ancestral language. In this book, we have conformed to this definition of etymology. We have traced a word to its 'earliest recorded occurrence', which in many cases happens to be Sanskrit. In doing this, there is no intention of claiming for Sanskrit the status of being the mother language; nor do we think less of the modern European languages because they are derived from their own old forms with close affinity to Sanskrit. Whatever be their past affiliations, a time came when they separated and struck independent paths and began to develop in their own specific ways, in response to their new environment. They incorporated new experiences, and expressed the psyche of their speakers under new influences, in new forms. They have now their own beauty and truth.

But even after this explanation if some people still prefer Indo-European roots, they are welcome. It will take away nothing from the central thesis of this book, nor compromise any of its arguments in any way. We ourselves have great respect for these roots, in spite of certain reservations into which we need not go here. A good deal of scholarship, skill and labour has gone into making them though perhaps the initial impulse was not purely scholarly. These roots were constructed at a time when Europe had to be the gracious dispenser of everything and Asia a grateful recipient. But when Europe discovered Sanskrit, a different kind of fact stared her in the face. Sanskrit's affinity with European languages, old or new, could not be denied; it was also the oldest of all known Aryan languages. So if there was any deriving or borrowing, it was in the other direction. But it was humiliating for European languages to own descent from an Asian source. So there was a motive in inventing something still older, preferably with a European home, from which Sanskrit as well as other allied languages could be derived. This made Sanskrit into a distant kinsman but not a direct ancestor. It was still unsatisfactory but it was the best that could be done under the circumstances.

There could be another objection. While the book aims at dealing with language as a human institution in its more universal aspect, it draws all its illustrative material from the Indo-European group of languages. This is due to the author's limitation, his lack of familiarity with non-Aryan languages. But if speech and meanings are deeply human phenomena and if they follow deeply-laid patterns of the mind and heart, then they must share certain common characteristics, however differently clothed, and certain truths must hold good for them all. This the scholars of different language-groups could test for themselves.

We have also to offer another necessary clarification. Because the book deals with words and their higher meanings and even refers to yoga and meditation, it could be confused with Śabda Yoga. There is a good deal of discussion of *śabda* (sounds) in Indian religious literature, particularly of the tantric persuasion. But the present volume is different both in its subject-matter as well as in approach. It deals with *logos*, with *vāk*, speech, the pregnant word, not with *dhvani* or *śabda*, sound. Its approach too is not esoteric. It does not eschew the logical and the known; but it uses them in a way that they stimulate love for the supra-logical and the supra-rational; it uses the known so that it points to the unknown. The unknown and supra-logical of this book, however, is not arbitrary and does not violate man's deeper reason and his larger sense of the truth.

As the discussion proceeds in the book, it shows how, beneath the surface meanings of a word, deeper meanings are hidden; how names of physical objects become names of concepts and qualities and how they, in turn, become names of psychic and spiritual truths, become names of Gods, become names of the truths of the Self. It also shows how these deepening meanings could be unearthed through alert and devout attention, called meditation in yogic literature.

Meditation has different meanings and different functions in different Yogas. It could be used for unfoldment and growth as well as for trance and ecstasy. It also makes use of different methods and techniques. Certain Yogas use certain sounds for concentration; other Yogas, knowing that mystic truths cannot be adequately expressed in conventional logic, propose certain illogical thoughts and puzzles, called *koans*, for reflection. The idea is to exhaust the mind as a preparation for a sudden jump into the great Void.

While these methods have their place and utility and are good for a certain kind of mind and for certain defined purposes, their limitations should be clearly understood and they should also not be conceived too mechanically. A baffled mind before God's or life's mystery is not the same thing as a mind consciously planning to get baffled with the help of a *koan*. Nor is a pacified and purified heart that has given up hankering the same thing as a mind lulled to a soothing inactivity by the hypnotic effect of a sound.

Meditation in this volume carries a different connotation. Meditation here means attention to sublime objects and meaningful and noble thoughts and words which increasingly reveal deeper, sublimer, and nobler meanings. Not the jump of a mind staggered by a *koan* to the paradoxes of a vast Puzzle or Pun or Jest or Conundrum, but the journey of an increasingly purified heart to the holy life and higher meanings of the Self.

According to the conclusion of this book, language is more than a mechanical tool. If we become aware of it, human speech is a great, sacred gift of God and expresses the deep, mysterious life of man's psyche, the same as temples, cathedrals, great music and great sculpture do. If the present work inculcates a feeling of reverence and holiness about our language and a sense that we should not abuse it, then its purpose will be served. We repeat, the book is not on language in the narrow sense of the term. It is about the deeper truths of the psyche and spirit; it is about the higher life as articulated in human speech; it is about Gods and their Names, which reveal increasingly deeper meanings and also become increasingly dynamic in life, through purity and dedication. It may interest many to know that Mahatma Gandhi, at an early stage in his life, had memorized the thousand Names of God; but this performance initially mnemonic became, through great inner searching and invoking, truths of his mind and heart, became Self-revelatory. In later life, he came to concentrate more and more on one Name, God as Truth, which became reversible for him in Truth as God. While the cultivation of one truth gave him the benefit of all other truths as well, it also taught him that truth of God is ultimately the truth of one's own secret Self.

We owe a great deal to Sir M. Monier-Williams' *Sanskrit-English Dictionary*, to Rev. W.W. Skeat's *Etymological Dictionary of English Language*, to Eric Partridge's *Origins*, to *Webster's Seventh New Collegiate Dictionary*, and to the *Shorter Oxford English Dictionary*. We contributed the direction, the logic, the pattern and the arguments, but these volumes provided the material for the embroidery, the necessary scholarship and authenticity; in short, the body and blood to the soul of the book.

For the English renderings of the Sanskrit texts, we have mostly used H.H. Wilson's and R.T.H. Griffith's translations of the *Ṛgveda*, R.E. Hume's translation of *The Thirteen Principal Upanishads*, and Annie Besant and Bhagavan Das's translation of the *Bhagavadgītā*.

At the end, we would like to thank friends who contributed in making this book what it is. We would mention in particular the names of Shri A.B. Chatterjee, Shri H.P. Lohia, Mr. James Michaels, Dr. Raimundo Panikkar, Shri and Shrimati Gautam Dharmapal, Dr. Uno Remitz, Dr. Govind Gopal Mukhopadhyaya, Shri Som Benegal, Dr. Mukund Lath, Dr. Wolfgang Somary,

Madame Vesna Krmpotic, Shri S.B. Roy, Shri Balkrishna Rao, Shri Surendra Saxena, Dr. Gita Dharampal, Shri Vasudeva Poddar, and Mrs. Irene Ray.

Some of these friends helped in ways that cannot easily be spelled out; the contribution of others was more palpable. They all read the manuscript, many of them in its first version, and gave it a generous welcome. They also found it useful. Dr. Remitz, for example, said that after reading the book, Gods for him became living and acquired a reality which they did not have before; Dr. Somary and Dr. Peter Schreiner said that the book helped them to have a better understanding of the Hindu concept of Gods. All this placed us under a moral obligation to put in necessary effort and make the manuscript ready for publication.

Dr. R. Panikkar went through the first draft carefully and made valued comments. He helped both by saying as well as not saying certain things. Other friends helped in more concrete ways. Mukund Lath and Gauri Dharmapal checked the Sanskrit texts; Mrs Irene Ray, without accepting larger editorial responsibilities for lack of time, yet suggested many editorial improvements. Vijayan and Rajan did the typing.

My friend Sita Ram Goel, scholar and publisher, was associated with the preparation of the manuscript in its various stages. In a way, the book belongs to him. He also prepared the Glossary and the Index. The Glossary gives important Sanskrit terms used in the text; the Sanskrit Names of Gods, mostly concentrated in Chapter XII, have been omitted.

The widely accepted scheme of transliteration has been used for rendering Sanskrit sounds into the Roman script. But for the sake of smooth reading popular spellings of certain words like Sanskrit, Vedic, Krishna, Vishnu and Shiva, already well-established in the English language, have been retained except when they appear in a learned context.

RAM SWARUP

Kṛṣṇa Janmaṣṭamī, Saṃvat 2037
September 2, 1980

G-3, Maharani Bagh,
New Delhi 110 065

Part One

CHAPTER 1

The Speech-sounds

How do words arise? What is their source? Where do they come from? Which are earlier, things or names? Are words merely labels? Or do they express, in some way, the essence of the things they name? Is onomastics, a scientific study of the origin and forms of words and names, possible?

At first sight, these questions appear to be simple to answer and useless to raise. Man is a social being. He has fears to express, a mate or mates to attract. He has to warn, to make signs, to show off, in order to survive. Given some intelligence and organs of articulation beyond those of brutes, it is obvious that man should invent some kind of a system of signs to facilitate mutual communication.

In any case, what is this question of primacy of words or things? Is it not obvious that things come first and their names come afterwards? Things are real; words are airy. That which we call a rose, by another name will smell as sweet. We use a small portion of our speech to give names to even a smaller portion of the things of the world. There are an infinite number of things in the womb of time and far-away spaces waiting to be named, just as there are things, images and emotions in our minds and hearts without a name and a local habitation. But the lack of names does not diminish their reality or importance. Names are an accident—and, some would say, an unhappy accident—in the life of mankind. Animals manage to live without a word-language and consequently without wars and propaganda and lying commercials and ads. Man too has lived without a language or, at least, with a very rudimentary form of it, in the past. He may do so again in future when either because he has descended to a new barbarism as a result of internecine wars or because he has so evolved that the present plethora and babel of names, made up of words of dubious and imprecise meanings, gives place to exact mathematical signs and equations.

In any case, what do we gain by raising the question? What is its utility? Man's language is given and that is the end of it. We might discuss the grammar, syntax, structure and peculiarities of a language but any discussion beyond that, into its so-called deeper origin and significance, can only be an idle speculation.

But the question is not as simple as that. Those who have given thought to this subject have found in speech and words a deep mystery. To all appearances, a word melts or evaporates into thin air as soon as it is spoken but in reality it has a subtle, inner life. A word is like a thought, seemingly insubstantial but in reality incarnating a deep truth of mind, life, and consciousness. Words change and even melt and die but when we go behind appearances we find that they have seed or core meanings which persist through time's ups and downs, wear and tear.

It is widely admitted that speech and psyche are intimately connected. Therefore, the question has great meaning for those who are attracted by the need of self-discovery. Any apparent lack of utility of this study will not deter a serious inquirer. If mind and speech are closely linked, it will be a great thing to understand this link and feel the innerness of speech. Then speech will no longer remain an outer ornament or even a utilitarian tool invented to facilitate a certain purpose. Rather, it will seem to take birth and grow from some inner, psychic centre or centres. Language will no longer be a collection of disparate words and signs, but something like a tree, its different parts coming out of a common root, and held together in the unity of mind. It will no longer be the mind's tool or invention, accidental, arbitrary and detachable, but its indispensable expression, necessary and inevitable.

It is obvious that the problem which we have set out to study is not an easy one. It involves exploration beyond the frontiers of the mind in that twilight zone or rarified atmosphere where thought tends to cease and melts into silence. The study calls for patience and intuitive feeling, for forces and processes which are subtle, which lie behind the outer appearances of things.

Apart from the prospect of gaining knowledge of some important facet of our mind, we have also another aim in making this enquiry. Hard is the knowledge of the good and names are a great part of that knowledge, believes Plato. Our purpose is to understand that aspect of the language in which it incarnates the higher reaches of mind, and expresses the deeper truths of the heart.

Language has not merely expressed man's fears; it has also expressed his sense of mystery. Again and again, man has sung of Gods and Divine Life and his idea of the Good and the Beautiful in sublime speech. This sublime speech, these inspired words, he has treasured as his veritable heritage, his Vedas. But in the passage of time, man's thought-habits and speech-mores change and the inspired words become difficult to understand. Can a study of language, in the manner we have indicated, help us to recapture the meanings of older scriptures? Can this study help us to understand the deeper life of man, his vision of Gods and the Good? Can this study throw some light on religious consciousness in general and the cherished old scriptures in particular? For example, can we understand the mentality of the seers of the Vedas—humanity's oldest extant scripture—by studying their language? Or can we understand the import of their language by entering into the state of their mind?

This kind of enquiry is particularly important at a time when there is a general distrust of words. The distrust comes not only from logical positivists but also from preachers who claim to teach higher truths. A reasonable warning against the misuse of words and language is apt and necessary. The 'letter killeth' was stressed by all teachers. But some new teachers go to absurd lengths in denouncing all scriptures. In fact, at times it appears that their only claim to religious leadership consists in their sweeping denunciation of scriptures. Their teaching is steeped in negativism and denial but in the process they create their own scriptures for their own followers.

II

The best way to begin the inquiry is to refer to a dialogue by Plato, *Cratylus*, in which he discusses this very problem with a view to understand the mystery of speech. He does not claim to have solved the mystery, but he does succeed in deepening the enquiry and in making several valuable suggestions. In this dialogue, one character, Hermogenus, doubts if "there is any principle of correctness in names other than convention or agreement".[1] Another character, Cratylus, from whom the dialogue takes its name, holds that things have names by nature or, at least, names have by nature a truth to express, and, though not everyone knows how to give a true name, nor are things and men always called by their true names, there is a truth and correctness in names which do express the forms of things and which is the same for the Hellenes as well as for the barbarians.

Socrates agrees with the second position and shows why. Let us, he says, suppose that we had no voice or tongue, but we wanted to communicate. Then like the deaf and dumb, we should imitate the nature of things with our hands and head and the rest of the body: the elevation of our hands to heaven to express highness and upwardness; letting things drop down to the ground for heaviness and drowsiness. So as limbs imitate things in order to express them,[2] similarly, in some subtle way, words and vocables also imitate things to express them.

---

[1]*Cratylus*, 384, *The Dialogues of Plato* translated by B. Jowett.

[2]All languages have a system of signs made up of bodily gestures. We have gestures of approval, appreciation, anger, disapproval, fear, repentance, distress, beckoning, obscenity. We speak, threaten, supplicate, greet and pray with our hands, face and eyes, and vote with our feet. These gestures go into the making of many phrases in a language. In English we have, nodding or shaking the head, turning up one's nose, shaking the fist in defiance, holding one's head high, winking, pouting, pulling a long face, face to face, eye to eye, shoulder to shoulder. There are phrases like highbrow, browbeat, underhand, warm-hearted, eye-opener, eyeful, ear-splitting, prick up one's ears, elbow one's way, cold-shoulder, faceless, glad eye, hand in hand. The last phrase has a perfect Chinese equivalent in which two hands are shown together to designate a 'friend'.

In this connection, read a very interesting article, 'Gesture' by F.C. Hayes, in ...

Socrates explains the point further. He says that as all objects have sound and figure and may have colours too and the arts which are concerned with them are music and drawing; similarly each thing has an essence too which could be expressed in letters and syllables.

Socrates says that we must first break a word into its primary letters. Just as a musician first considers the power of elementary and then of compound sounds and then proceeds to the consideration of rhythm, similarly, we must separate vowels and consonants and mutes and then see whether they imitate things of nature. On considering this he finds they do.

Like ancient Indian thinkers on the subject, Socrates also finds that the sound *rh* (letter *rho*) expresses motion and that it is an excellent instrument for the expression of that idea. In this sound, primitive men observed that "the tongue was most agitated and least at rest". Therefore, it is actually used in words which mean flowing, trembling, striking, crushing, breaking, bruising, crumbling, whirling. Similarly, in pronouncing sounds represented by letters *psi, phi, sigma* and *zeta,* there is a great expenditure of breath; therefore, they are used in the imitation of notions like shivering (*psukhron*) and seething (*zeon*). The sound *n* seems to be sounded from within and, therefore, to have a notion of inwardness. Hence, we find this sound in words like *endon* (in, within), and *entos* (inside, within). The sound *l* has a liquid quality and, in pronouncing it, the tongue seems to slip; therefore, it is found in words which mean smooth, level, sleek and slip. *Alpha* is the best for the expression of size, *eta* for length, because "they are

---

... the *Encyclopedia Americana*. The article mentions for the Spanish language a dictionary, *Diccionario de Modismos*, which lists nearly 300 phrases in which the hand alone figures. Similarly, for the English language also, a small dictionary like the *Webster's New World Dictionary*, gives more than 70 uses for the word hand, 58 for foot, 35 for face, 57 for eye, and 32 for nose.

The Indian classical dance has perfected this gestural language. Through it, it expresses very mood or *bhāva*, relates stories from the epics, expresses some of the highest ideas. In fact, sometimes this gestural language could be most economical, most eloquent. A seated Buddha, a Tribhaṅgī Kṛṣṇa, or a Tāṇḍava Śiva tells more than whole volumes of books.

great letters". The *o* sound is round; therefore, it is found in words that mean roundness.[3]

So, according to Socrates, speech should be broken up into its elemental constituent-sounds which according to him have different expressive values. Socrates does not develop his suggestion and merely takes up individual words and names, mostly of Gods and moral qualities, for his illustration and elucidation. Therefore, we are left to fend for ourselves and see what we can make of this suggestion. But before we take up this point again, let us look a little more closely at the speech-sounds of a language.

III

There are about 3,000 languages in the world, two-thirds of them spoken by only a few thousand or even a few hundred people. Twelve languages—Chinese, Hindi, English, Russian, Spanish, German, Japanese, French, Italian, Malayan, Portuguese and Arabic—together cover an overwhelming majority of the world's population. Even these languages belong to larger language-groupings. For example, eight of them belong to the Indo-Aryan group of languages with many points of contact between them.

One would have thought that in these languages we would find a vast number of man's possible speech-sounds which, theoretically, are limitless. But in reality, all language-groups in the world have between them no more than a thousand sounds. Normally, the speech-sounds in any language never exceed sixty.

The English language has only 26 letters, though they do the work of 55 phonemes including 21 vowel sounds. A phoneme is the smallest unit of speech that serves to distinguish one utterance from another in a language. One language may make distinctions which another disregards; hence different languages have different phonemes.

In classical Sanskrit there are 48 articulate sounds, including 13 vowels (not counting *pluta* or protracted vowels), and

[3]*Cratylus*, 426-7.

35 consonants. Besides these, the Vedic language had two more sounds. It also divided vowels into *udātta* (acute), *anudātta* (grave) and *svarita* (circumflex).

In 1919 the Chinese Ministry of Education brought out a set of 39 phonetic letters. Most of these have their equivalents in Indo-European languages, though their clustering to form words is different in the Chinese language. Also, besides consonants and vowels, a Chinese word has a third constituent—a tone.

The Japanese language too has a simple phonetic structure. It has 5 vowels and 19 consonants. Vowels can be lengthened or combined to make diphthongs and some of the consonants change their sound-value in association with other sounds.

Even these 50 or 60 speech-sounds which a language uses are not all used equally. The potentiality of some sounds is exploited more fully than that of others. Some of them are used intensively, others sparingly, and yet others rarely if at all.

In the English language, the letters *e, t, a, o, n, i, r, s,* and *h* belong to the high-frequency group. These nine letters between them account for 70 per cent frequency, that is, in a passage containing 100 letters, 70 of them are likely to be these nine. The letters *d, l, u, c* and *m* belong to the medium-frequency group, accounting for 16.5 per cent frequency. The letters *p, f, y, w, g, b,* and *v* belong to the low-frequency group of only 11.5 per cent. The letters *j, k, q, x* and *z* belong to the rare-frequency group, accounting for only 2 per cent.

This picture is somewhat inaccurate since we have given the frequency-use of different letters rather than of different sounds, which do not coincide in the English language. The letter *e* which represents the highest frequency, namely 13 per cent, could represent more than one sound and could also be represented in more than one way. It could be represented in 16 different ways, by *ee* as in fee, *ea* as in eat, *ie* as in mien, *ei* as in seize, *ey* as in key, *eo* as in people, *i* as in pin. Similarly, the sound *sh* in she is represented in several ways in words like sure, mission, Asia, issue, nausea, special, ocean, machine, conscience, schedule, anxious. But we hope that the two tendencies, one letter standing for several sounds and several letters expressing the same sound, cancel each other out and our frequency chart is broadly true of sound-values.

Dr. Gauri Dharmapal was kind enough to prepare for me the frequency-chart of Sanskrit letters as they appear in the *ślokas* 11-30 of the Second Chapter of the *Gītā*. From this we find that the letters *a, t, ā, n, i, y, v, r, e, s*, and *m* belong to the high-frequency group. Even within this group *a,* which tops the list, has two and a half times the frequency of *t,* the second in order, and almost eight times the frequency of letter *m,* the last in order. Letters *ṃ, ś, o, d, h, u, c, p, ḥ, k, bh, ī, j, ṇ, th, ṣ,* and *ai* belong to the medium-frequency group, the first of these being four times more frequent than the last. Letters *dh, ū, ṛ, au* belong to the low-frequency category; and the rest to the rare-frequency group including the cerebral mutes which are even rarer. Here one may also refer to the frequency-chart given by Dr. W.D. Whitney in his *Sanskrit Grammar*, commuted from a larger selection of passages drawn from literature of different categories and different epochs. The point all these charts make is that, though a language uses many speech-sounds, it does not attach the same importance to all of them.

Not only do sounds occur with different frequency, but they also associate differently and appear in different combinations and clusters in different languages. For example, *io* may be more frequent in one language, *oi* in another. Similarly, some letters may appear more frequently in the beginning than in the middle or at the end of the words. Frequency, place, and grouping of sounds tell a lot and influence the quality of a language and, perhaps, also enter into the meanings and associations of words.

All these sounds are divided into two kinds: vowels and consonants, as we have already seen. Vowel sounds are spoken primarily with the help of the larynx. Consonants, on the other hand, are formed in the cavity of the mouth above the larynx with the help of the palate, roof of the mouth, teeth and lips. These are called the organs of articulation. Consonants themselves are divided into guttural, palatal, cerebral, dental, and labial groups, each group taking its name after the organ which helps to produce the sound. So all manifest speech is characterized by constriction, by closure, at one or more points in the breath channel.

All these sounds have their individual qualities. Some are hard, some soft, some nasal, some sibilant. Some are short, some long, and yet others still more protracted. Some are acute, some grave, some aspirated, some voiced. Some are sharp, penetrating, hissing while others are deep and resonant. Some require a complete stoppage or closure of the organ of articulation, others do not. In pronouncing *a* in car, the size of the mouth-opening is five times that of pronouncing the sound *u* in moon. All vowels and some of the consonants like *l, m, n, r, s, z* can be prolonged indefinitely; but sounds like *b, p, t, d, k, g* cannot be prolonged. They are produced by completely stopping the exhaled column of air at three points. They are of extremely brief duration. But there are others of longer duration. They are called continuants, spirants, or fricatives.

Some sounds roll in the mouth, others reverberate. Some are round. Each sound has its peculiar stress and accent.

Besides these qualities, the speech-sounds also carry a subtle atmosphere of their own. They have movement, warmth, vibration, aura—even temper, personality and character.[4]

---

[4]In Sanskrit literature, according to certain theories of rhetoric, syllables express particular flavours, *rasas*. Cerebrals (*ṭ, ṭh, ḍ, ḍh, ṇ, ś* and *ṣ*) express virile sentiments; so do the first and the third syllables of different *vargas* (*k g, c j, ṭ ḍ, p b*) when combined with their second and fourth syllables (*kh, gh, ch, jh, ṭh, ḍh, ph, bh*) and accompanied by *r* before or after. Compound words intensify the sense of the virile sentiments.

On the other hand, the first four syllables of different *vargas* (except for the cerebrals which ought to be avoided altogether), when combined with their nasals (*ṅ, ñ, ṇ, m*) express softer sentiments. Even *r* and *ṇ*, when they are whole and simple to pronounce, do the same. Too many compound words have the opposite effect according to *Sāhitya Darpaṇa*.

The syllables have even their 'sex' and 'caste' according to the Tantras. Vowels and simple consonants are female; sibilants and aspirates are neutrals; gutturals are priestly; cerebrals, palatals, and dentals are warriors; labials and liquid are traders; sibilants and aspirates are workers. Gutturals are used for invoking Gods; palatals and dentals for giving call to action; labials and liquids for propitiation and persuasion; sibilants and aspirates are used in certain forms of black magic.

IV

This seems close to the view of Socrates and to support his thesis. In this view, speech-sounds are not merely physical; they represent psychic qualities, even ideas, which enter into the making of a name. How it happens, we do not know. Perhaps in giving names to objects and notions we choose, by an unconscious process, speech-sounds of such qualities as also render the qualities of their referents.

The idea is interesting but not without serious gaps. Could we really derive the rich vocabulary of a language with its hundreds of thousands of words from such a limited base of meanings? The meanings—if we can really call them so at this stage—of speech-sounds are general but those of names specific. Perhaps the qualities of speech-sounds could lend a particular character to a language, and give it a certain ethos, but that they could give a whole or a major part of the vocabulary will need a good deal of proving.

There is a cruder but more popular version of this theory which also derives the names of things from 'sounds' but not in the same way. In the Socratic view, sounds have qualities and meanings which they try to match with the qualities and meanings of objects. In the other view, speech-sounds have no such active and dignified status. In this view, names are echoic; they derive from vocal imitation of the sounds associated with things and actions named. Not only words like buzz, hiss, click, crack, creak, croak, crash, gnash but also words like pigeon, pipe, chirp, hark are considered imitative in origin. A language has hundreds of words of this kind.

But even this must be regarded as an insufficient explanation. Firstly, because not all things, actions, and ideas have sounds of the kind which could be physically reproduced, though some of these ideas and things could be very eloquent in another sense of the term. So, how could their sounds be imitated when they have no such sounds in the accepted sense of the term?

Secondly, a sound seems to adjust itself to any fact, object or experience. Some say a pig is a pig because it is so dirty. But if we reflect over the matter a little, we would find that the word pig smells not because of its sound but because of its referent. Headache to a Bengali sounds like *jhan-jhan;* to a Hindi-speaking person, it also sounds like *bhan-bhan. Tak-take lāl,* flashing red, seems to a Bengali to translate in the language of the sound a deeply held quality of the colour red—(or perhaps it is not a true imitative word at all, but merely tries to name a striking quality by a striking word)—but it does not seem so to non-Bengalis. The same is true of many other Bengali phrases like *cak-cake-roddur* (bright sunshine), *jhak-jhake ālo* (dazzling light), *phur-phure habā* (gentle breeze).

Thus it would appear that a speech-sound does not bring any quality or meaning to a name; on the other hand, it derives its quality from the thing named. Or at most one could say that a name and its referent absorb each other's qualities and meanings by a process of osmosis. They live in a kind of give-and-take and tend to be coequal. Like water, which takes on the form of the vessel in which it is poured, a sound takes on the shape, colour, and smell of the object it stands for. A sound is *vastusārupyam*; it takes on the form of the thing it stands for.

Thirdly, speech is more than grunts, hums, hoots, wails, cackles, chuckles, snorts, squeaks, giggles, and gnashings of teeth. These may explain words for an elementary and primitive order of life, but not words standing for the higher reaches of life, mind and intellect.

Thus onomatopoeia does not go very far in explaining the origin of names. It also offers little help to the views of Socrates. In fact, in certain essentials, it distorts them. In onomatopoeia, speech-sounds are no more than what they appear to the physical ear; in the thinking of Socrates, they are ideas, powers, and expressions of the mind. In the echoic theory, the name of a thing consists in the vocal imitation of the sound associated with it. To Socrates, this gives no true name. "People who imitate sheep, or cocks, or other animals" are not naming them, he says. Yet he does not rule out imitation altogether; only it means a different thing in the context of his thinking. There, a word does not imitate the sound of a thing, it imitates its 'form' or 'essence'; it expresses "the essence of each thing in letters and syllables", as he says.[5]

What should we understand by these statements? Socrates seems to say that every speech-sound has a specific idea to convey, however general; and when this idea also agrees with the idea conveyed by an object or action, we have a true name. For example, the sound *r* suggests, according to him, as we have already seen, the idea of motion; and he gives several words in his tongue which contain this sound and also mean motion or things in motion. This is how names are given by true legislators, or if we prefer to put it in more impersonal terms, come into being through the operation of an unconscious wisdom.

But this position too is not without its objections. Firstly, if *r* has such an unalterable meaning and quality, it must show it not only in the Greek language but in every other language too. Secondly, in any language including the Greek, there are words suggesting the meaning of movement but incorporating different speech-sounds. Go, walk, move, jump, fly, glide, come, spin, amble, evolve, descend, ascend are some examples in the English language. Similarly, a sound could enter into words meaning the same general idea but it could also enter into words meaning quite opposite ideas. For example, the sound *r* enters both into run as well as rest, the two standing for opposite ideas. Thus it seems to be difficult to find a visible correspondence between a system of speech-sounds and a system of objects and ideas, broad or detailed. Can we meet this objection?

Also, what to make of Socrates' other suggestion that names express the forms and essences of things? How do they do it? And what exactly does it mean? Socrates himself does not adequately discuss these questions. But perhaps his suggestions could acquire clarity and depth by referring to the Hindu thought on the subject.

V

The old Hindu seers had reflected deeply on many important questions concerning man, his being, his world, his speech.

---

[5]*Cratylus*, 423.

According to them, whenever the mind thinks of anything, it also invokes its corresponding form. The form has an essential sound or name attached to it. In fact, according to these seers, all phenomenal existence is *nāma-rūpa,* names and forms. Of these two, names are even more important than forms. An object is merely an outer expression, a material representation of the more internal and essential *nāma.*

The Hindus had also a well-developed theory of speech, *vāk.* According to this theory, speech exists at various levels, in different modes, and in different states of subtlety. Beyond the ordinary spoken level, it also exists as thought, as seed ideas. At these levels, it also includes within itself the objects and actions it names.

But before we take up this theory and look at it more closely, let us first see what the modern scientists have to say about speech.

According to the science of Acoustics, speech, as we ordinarily use it, is multiplied 300 times by the resonant effect of the larynx as the sound passes through it. Similarly, sounds become articulate speech as they pass through different organs of articulation like the tongue, palate, teeth, lips, when the air passes through the cavity of the mouth.

So, in a way, the basic sounds, the articulate speech-sounds as indicated by the syllabary or letters of a language, are not as self-sufficient as we thought them to be.

So, where do the sounds reside before they acquire audibility and amplitude through the larynx and articulation through the cavity of the mouth, and become modified into guttural, palatal, cerebral, dental, and labial sounds? The only valid assumption is that they exist as incipient speech, as prefiguration of speech and not the actual speech as we know it. In this state, speech is probably held in an undifferentiated form; at least, it cannot have the kind of differences that we know and infer from ordinary speech-sounds. At this stage, speech and words must reside in the mind as inclinations or intentions.

Also, at this stage, the sounds are not distinct; and yet the principle of distinction must be there in a seed form. For, what the larynx and the mouth-cavity add is acoustics, volume, audibility, vocability and articulation. But the spirit, the principle of discrimination, the principle of unity and difference must be there working all the time from behind. The differences in speech-sounds are most likely there, but they are, at this stage, held in abeyance.

Some of the activities beneath the threshold of the conscious mind, almost physiological and nervous in nature, have recently been recorded by the growing science of electronics. It has been found that the afferent and the efferent parts of the physiology of the human brain, or man's receptive and expressive centres are intimately related. Whenever a man sees or hears anything, he also tries to imitate it, reproduce it and express it in one form or another. Afferent sensations start efferent impulses. Any act of perception sets up a nervous tension which seeks release through expression. So every act of cognition invokes a mental disposition which expresses itself in some lingual form.

Though this proclivity alone will not explain the birth of a word or name, it is obvious that the sound exists at a more subtle level than we ordinarily know. Even at the level of empiricism and scientific experiments, it exists at least at two levels—audible and inaudible, obvious and relatively hidden, manifest and relatively unmanifest.

But the Indian sages go further and enumerate four levels of speech of increasing subtlity—*vaikharī*, *madhyamā*, *paśyantī* and *parā*. The *vaikharī* level is the level that we ordinarily know, where the sound is formed, *śabda-niṣpatti*. Its seat is the throat. Behind it, and supporting it, is the *madhyamā vāk* with its seat in the heart region. It cannot be heard by all but the more attentive can hear it by closing their ears. It can always be heard by the inner ear, *śrutigocara*. Here the sequence and form, *kramarūpa*, are not the same as we see them in ordinary speech. Beyond this lie two other levels, *paśyantī* and *parā,* with their seats at the navel, *nābhi,* and the solar plexus, *mūlādhāra,* respectively. They are beyond the ken of the ordinary mind and they can be seen only by

Yogis in states of deep trance. In *paśyantī,* there is no sound but only meaning, *dyotitārtha.* In this state, the speech is indivisible, *avibhāga*, and the forms and sequence are fused or concentrated, *sarvataḥ saṃhṛta-krama*, as in a seed. In *parā* the speech is established in its own luminous form, *svarūpajyotiḥ*, and in its original, primal form before any modifications start. Here sound becomes silence, *aśabda,* and only a potentiality, *avyakta.*

But between this noumenal and essential existence of a sound at the unmanifest level and the sound on the phenomenal and manifest level, there are many steps and many processes. According to Pāṇini's *Śikṣā*, quoted by Mrs. Annie Besant and Dr. Bhagavan Das, the Self first cognizes and formulates intentions by means of *buddhi*; then it inspires *manas* with desire to speak; *manas* strikes *kāyāgni*, body-fire or nerve-force; that, in turn, sets in motion *marut,* wind or breath; which first moves to the chest, then rises to the palate and finally passes to the mouth, producing articulate sounds classified according to tone, time, place and effort.[6]

But the meaning of a word does not reside in this last, visible part, in the spoken and audible, fourth limb of a word; rather, it resides in the subtlest portion of the word, in that condition of a sound which, as we have seen, is different from and beyond the syllables, *varṇātirikta*, but still manifested by them. In this status, the word is without any outward expression, without any vocal limbs, *niravayava*, is permanent, *nitya*. Indeed, in this status, it is the cause of the world, *jagannidānam*, and is Brahman Itself.

But for those whom this kind of speculation does not interest and also for our immediate purpose it is not necessary to go this far with the Hindus. It is enough to recognize the next subtle level which a little introspection on our own part can reveal and which scientific instruments can measure. It is enough to say that sounds exist at two levels—as speech-sounds as we ordinarily know

---

[6]The *Bhagvad Gita* translated by Annie Besant and Bhagavan Das, 6th Edition, Adyar, 1973, p. xxi.

them, as guttural, palatal, cerebral, dental or labial; and on the more subtle, unmanifest level, where these distinctions are still in abeyance.

This could meet the objection to Socrates' theory that different sounds could not stand for different specific ideas as all kinds of ideas are expressed by all kinds of speech-sounds in different languages and even in the same language. For, at the subtle level, a sound represents the general essence of several sounds at the same time. It exists in a form where it could be expressed by different speech-sounds and syllables at the same time. At this level, the sound is not labial or dental or palatal or cerebral or larynxial, yet it could be represented by any such sound without making any difference.

This fact may explain why there are different words for the same thing or the same or similar sounds to express different things and ideas in different languages and in the same language. At the subtle, essential level, the sound to express a particular object or idea is the same; but at the gross, phenomenal level, its forms and disguises could change from language to language and even in the same language. The essential sound could stand for several phenomenal sounds. A race chooses one sound rather than another according to its own genius, inclination, growth, and law of *karma*. A language develops the potentiality of a seed sound according to its genius and capacity.

In his discussion, Socrates also reaches a point where he too draws the same conclusion but he does not pursue the subject far enough. He gives the simile of smiths who do not use the same iron in making instruments for the same purpose; but as long as the 'form' is the same, the instrument must be good even though the material varies and the smith himself may be a barbarian. Similarly, a name-giver, whether he be a Hellene or a barbarian, is to be deemed wise, "provided he gives the true and proper form of the name in *whatever syllables*".[7]

So even according to Socrates, there is something more to a

---

[7]*Cratylus*, 389-90. Emphasis added.

word than its syllables or outer sound. Its true meaning resides in its proper 'form', which lies beyond its syllables.

VI

The above theory may explain that a subtle sound represents several speech-sounds but the question still remains: how do sounds whether subtle or gross represent the attributes of things and objects?

We have already answered the question by implication but let us now do it more explicitly and expressly. Let us also attempt our answer in the language of Sāṃkhya. According to Sāṃkhya, the world derives from the *mūla-prakṛti,* inadequately translated as Nature in English. *Prakṛti* in its downward evolution towards manifoldness, at one stage takes to two paths. With that quality which is called *sattva*, in which light predominates, it becomes the subjective world. With this part it creates the *antaḥkaraṇa*, the *buddhi,* the *ahaṃkāra*, the *manas,* the senses. With the other quality called *tamas*, translated as darkness, it becomes the objective world, the world of *tanmātrās*, and the five elements. So, Janus-like, *prakṛti* is two-faced, one face turned towards the subject and the other towards the object.[8] But the two worlds, seemingly opposed, are not different; they are aspects of the same original reality. They take their birth from the same womb. They are involved in each other and they leave their echo and image and vibrations behind in each other. We could, therefore, probably reasonably conclude that the sound at its subtle level expresses the

---

[8]The old seers always discovered an intimate relationship between different orders of Reality. The Upanishads always established correspondences between the inner and the outer, the cosmic and the individual, the higher and the lower, between the *ādhidaivika* and the *ādhibhautika* and the *ādhyātmika*. For example, they linked Eye and the Sun, Speech and Fire, Breath and Wind, Mind and Moon. (*Chāndogya Upaniṣad*, 3.18)

These pairs meet and mingle constantly. They originate in each other and go back into each other. Yājñavalkya says that the voice of a dead man goes into fire, his breath into wind, his eyes into the sun, his mind into the moon, his hearing into the quarters of heaven, his body into the earth, his soul into space. (*Bṛhadāraṇyaka Upaniṣad*, 3.2.13)

subtle vibrations and qualities of an object. At this subtle level, the two pick up and enter into the vibrations of each other. The *vaikharī* sound represents the body, the physical vestment of a word. But the subtle sound, the soundless sound in the word, represents the soul, the inner meaning. The first is subject to change, to the wear and tear of time; the second is permanent. The second does not change when the first changes nor ceases to represent it.

But due to one reason or another a word may lose its inwardness or it may have been invented to represent a thing's more outward appearances and qualities; in such cases the word will be a shell, a body without soul. Every language has plenty of such words.

This may also explain Socrates' observation that not all things are known by their true names. Every idea has a true form and an appropriate sound. But as nations become unresponsive to the inwardness of things, they may lose the capacity of knowing things in their true forms and knowing their true names and sounds. They only know a thing by its outermost aspect, and therefore by its outermost form and name. Increasingly, they live in a shadow-world, made of shadow-ideas, expressing shadow-forms and shadow-names. Perhaps our intuition that names do not represent things but are artificial labels is true in this sense. We live in the midst of shadows of things, names and forms, not with true things and forms and names.

CHAPTER 2

How New Things are Named

There may be something in the above theory of sound, but many would have preferred a less speculative and more empirical treatment of the subject.

In that case, the best way would be to see how names are given in our own times. Name-giving is not something which took place long ago in the beginning of things. It is taking place even now. New words are constantly taking birth. The *Oxford English Dictionary* has recently published a Supplement which is not yet complete. From A to G, it gives 18,000 words with 30,000 different meanings that have been accepted into the English language in the last 100 years. New experiences, new things, new concepts call for new names. Let us take certain new concrete facts like a motor car, a telephone, a telescope, a telegraph, an aeroplane, an aeronaut or astronaut or pilot, etc. They have come into being only lately. Let us see how they have been named.

The process is something like this. Suppose some new concept or idea appears on the horizon and calls for a new name; then we review our old experience to find something in it to characterize the new. Probably we have a number of words to choose from. Then one of those words with suitable modifications could be used to describe the new fact; another retained to express the old. This is possible because, at heart, the new facts themselves have some kind of unity with the old. Words express this unity of experience. In due course, the two words would acquire shades of meaning which they did not have before.

Now take motor cars and let us see how they were named. 'Car' is an old word. In the Celtic language, it was *karr*, a chariot; in the Irish language *carr*, a cart. The German (Ger.) *karre* also meant the same thing. It is also allied to Latin (L.) *currus*, a chariot. So car was an old word which first described a cart, a barrow or a chariot, then began to describe the new transport. In the process, it also gave birth to many more words like career, cargo, charge, etc.

Thus car, cart, chariot, though they are from the same source, are now used to describe particular kinds of vehicles.

The word 'vehicle' itself is an old one. Through various intermediate stages, it could be traced to the Sanskrit (Skt.) root *vah*, to carry, which gives us the Skt. *vāhana*, a vehicle. This root is also the ancestor of several other modern words like way, wagon, envoy, voyage.

The same is true of the word 'telephone'. It derives from the Greek (Gk.) *tele*, afar off, and *phōnē*, voice or sound. *Phōnē* itself has probably and older cousin in Skt. *bhan*, to speak. So a telephone is 'distant speaking'; it now applies to the instrument which makes distant communication possible.

The words 'telescope' and 'telegram' have also a similar origin. 'Telescope' derives from the Gk. *tele*, afar off, and *skopein*, to behold, itself related to Skt. *paś* or *spaś*, to see. In 'telegraph', 'graph' derives from Gk. *graphein*, to write, to scratch. This root also gives us the modern English word 'carve', which shows that writing was once carving or, at least, that the two processes were intimately linked.

Now take another word 'airplane' or 'aeroplane' which is more popular in Great Britain. Here also the object is new but the name is old. The word is derived from two Greek words: *aēr*, air, and *planos*, wandering (which gives us another beautiful word 'planet' from *'planēt'* or *planēs*, a wanderer). So, an aeroplane means a wanderer in the sky. But it could as well have received a name from any root which gives us words like 'eagle', 'kite', or 'bird'. In fact, in some dialects of India, an aeroplane is called *cīla gāḍi,* a kite vehicle. Indonesia has named its international air services after Garuḍa, the divine king of birds in Hindu mythology.

The word 'aeronaut' which means one who travels by or operates an airship derives from Gk. *aēr*, air, and *nautēs*, sailor, from *naus*, a ship. A ship or boat is also *nau* in Sanskrit.

'Aeronaut' has a synonym in 'astronaut'. It derives from L. *astrum*, Gk. *astron*, Skt. *tārā*, all meaning a star. So an astronaut means a traveller in interplanetary space.

But the two words have not been able to replace the older one, 'pilot', which still continues to be popular. 'Pilot' derives from Gk. *peda*, steering oars. So probably the word originally meant a person who plied a country boat; then it began to refer to those employed to steer a ship. Now it applies to one who flies or is qualified to fly an aeroplane. Thus its use was extended from the maritime to the aeronautical.

II

Now from simple names of concrete things let us go to words of a different magnitude where they express social and psychological factors. Sometimes a word contains the history of the rise and fall of nations, classes, gods, ideologies, their conflicts and reconciliations, their clashes and dialectical movements, their pretence, reality and rationalization. It contains a good deal of historical and sociological data congealed in one place, which may not be available elsewhere.

Let us take words such as barter, exploit, capital, property, used in books on Economics; or names of classes like slaves, serfs, proletariat; or epithets like gentleman, *sāhib*, comrade, minister. These are all socially significant words and they will illustrate our point.

The word 'barter' now has the sense of exchange of goods. But, according to etymologists, its earlier form also meant 'to cheat', 'to beguile', 'to betray'. Not all exchange may be cheating but the word expresses a great human experience that exchange could be the vehicle of great cheating, even more than stray cases of outright snatching and robbing. In fact, nations and classes are cheated more through differential terms of trade and manipulated exchange rates than through direct human exploitation. Now, in most countries, there is no direct slave labour as such, but there are differential rates of remuneration and exchange which are unrelated to the intrinsic worth or value of different kinds of activities or labour, and as a result whole classes and nations are cheated. For example, the dollar-rupee exchange ratio is quite unrelated to the internal purchasing power of the two currencies. In America, a dollar will not buy goods worth more than two rupees in India but their exchange value does not reflect this fact. This is not fair trade.

Another word we very commonly hear these days is 'exploit'. Originally, the word had a good sense. It meant 'to achieve', 'to act with effect'. Next, it acquired a connected but lower meaning, 'to turn to account'—not to accountability but to profitability. In the last century, the word has acquired another meaning, 'to utilize for selfish purpose'. That is the nature of all *rājsika* (impure vital) movements. These lead to self-motivated use of others. Today, the exploitation of nature's resources is even more selfish and leads to greater dangers than the exploitation of labour.

Then we have the word 'capital'. It is a word of Latin origin and meant wealth, stock, worth, property. But in a pre-industrial age, the concept of wealth itself was different. Capital in those days mainly meant property in land, animals and even slaves. In fact, in due course, the word capital gave rise to a doublet, 'cattle', and 'chattel', which developed these senses more fully. 'Cattle' originally meant property in general, then it began to mean property in bovine animals. 'Chattel' acquired the added sense of a slave or a bondsman. Today, capital fulfills some of its old functions and answers to some of its old definitions in a new setting. In a way, it has not changed much in its relations and attitudes. Whether it is the soil or the hidden bowels of the mother earth or the elements of nature or God's other creatures or fellow-men, all are factors of production. All are for maximum use.

The next word 'property' is related to the words 'proper' and 'propriety'. It is from the L. *proprius*, one's own. Philosophically, it meant a quality or trait belonging and especially peculiar to an individual. So it meant a thing's true nature, or what makes it what it is, what differentiates it from others. This gave the word the sense of virtue, proper, fitting, righteous, appropriate. In India, the term used was *dharma*, quality, attribute, nature. From this, the word acquired a passive sense, 'something owned or possessed' or 'appropriated exclusively'. From this, in easy steps, the word acquired a more material meaning, 'a piece of real estate', or 'real estate to which a person has exclusive legal rights'.

Now take another word 'slave'. It is derived from *Slavs*, the Slavonic peoples of Central Europe. When they were captured and made bondsmen, they gave birth to the word 'slave'.

Gibbon, whom W.W. Skeat quotes, thought that the word was allied to Russian *slava*, which meant glory and fame; Eric Patridge thinks that the word literally meant 'the speaker' and hence an 'intelligent' person, as opposed to the Germans who were called 'the mutes'. But as fortunes changed, the word which once signified glory, fame and intelligence now signified servitude and meanness.

The word 'slave' also gave us the word 'serf'. Originally, 'serf' meant a slave in general from L. *seruus*, a slave; but during medieval times, it acquired the specifically feudal meaning of a bonded servant attached to the soil. The forces and relations of production change, but the dispossessed remain the same. The slaves became serfs and later on the same class provided the labour force for the factories under a different name.

This brings us to the word 'proletariat', which is very much in use these days. Now it means 'a class of industrial workers who lack their own means of production and hence sell their labour to live'. Under Marxist influence, it has also acquired an ideological meaning and, today, it may also mean the 'future' class, the class that will inherit the earth. But, historically, the word referred to those who belonged to the lowest class. The word derives from L. *proletārius,* a member of the lowest class, but useful for producing children (*proles*, progeny) for the state for military purposes. Later on, under the influence of Adam Smith, the contribution of this class was supposed to consist in providing labour to the industrial system at a subsistence level.

Now we take up different epithets or names by which people call themselves and call each other. The word 'gentleman' means a man of noble and generous character, some one polite, courteous and gallant. The word is derived from L. *gentīlis*, belonging to the same clan (Skt. *jan*, to beget), and hence good, noble and well-born. With the passage of time, the word acquired a class significance. It began to signify a man of independent means, a man who does not engage in any occupation or profession for gain. It also acquired a legal definition. Only those entitled to bear arms were called gentlemen.

But economic circumstances were changing and old classes were dying out. To belong to an upper class socially without its supporting income was bound to deflate the meaning of the word. And, hence, under new compulsions and also under the influence of new equalitarian concepts, the word in its older meaning is going out of fashion. It is now used to signify all male members of any social class or condition. Some even feel embarrassed if the word is applied to them. It has also come to mean, jocularly, a man without means of livelihood, a gentleman at large.

We have the word '*sāhib*' used in India for European rulers and for our own upper class. It is an Arabic word which originally meant a 'companion'. But when the Arabs became imperial rulers, the word acquired a different connotation. It began to mean 'master' or 'lord' and it still retains that meaning.

The word 'comrade' is undergoing a similar sea-change. It is derived from a Spanish word *camarada*, a cabin-mate, a tent-sharer, a companion. Within the Communist parties, the term was initially applied to the equals in struggle. But as the power equation changed and the rebels became rulers, the meaning of the word also changed. In Soviet Russia and other Communist countries, the word does not mean any cheek by jowl relationship or hail-fellow-well-met familiarity; on the other hand, it means something like 'lord' or 'ruler' to the common people, some one against whom you should be on your guard.

The word 'minister' is Latin in origin and it meant a servant, one who assisted another at a religious cult, hence a public officer, finally one at the head of a political department. It is in this sense that the word is used in India, as some one very important and privileged. There is also nothing very self-effacing and humble about a church minister in consonance with the lowly origin of the word. If any thing, he is even more pretentious. He administers the sacraments and saves souls; he is an official of the church, the sole channel of God's grace.

III

In the examples quoted above, one feature stands out prominently: that in no case a completely new word has to be invented to indicate a new fact or new object. An old word is found to name a new object. And like a living organism, the old responds to accommodate the new. If a new word is invented at all, the invention must be at a very different level hardly accessible to the ordinary perception.

In the process of challenge and response, a word sometimes suffers contraction in meaning and sometimes experiences expansion. Sometimes from a concrete and narrow sense, it acquires a more abstract and general meaning. Sometimes words from the same root develop different suggestions of the root and bifurcate in very different directions. Sometimes of two words of two different origins but meaning the same thing, one is taken up and the other dropped; or both are retained to indicate two different shades of the same general meaning.

For example, 'shop' in England meant a small retail establishment. In America, this meaning was replaced by the word 'store'. The word 'shop' itself took the meaning of a 'factory'. In the past, in the days of agricultural and cattle economy, the word had a different meaning than either a factory or even a store. It meant 'a shed for cattle' as in Anglo-Saxon *scypen*, or 'a shed, a cart-house' as in Ger. *schuppen*.

Take another word 'merchant'. It derives from L. *mercāri,* to barter, and came to mean a trader, a dealer in merchandise. This sense was retained in America but, in England, the word was restricted to apply to a wholesale trader especially with foreign countries. The change came when the merchants of the East India Company became rich. After that the name which they had hitherto shared with their less successful brother was not good enough to do justice to them both. So the word acquired a more exclusive connotation.

The word 'mercer' too has the same origin as the word 'merchant', but it too refers to a specialized trade. It denotes a dealer in textile fabrics.

The word 'corn' meant grain in general and especially wheat in England; but when it migrated to America, it began to mean 'maize'.

Similarly, the 'Government' in England was once known as 'Administration'. Now America uses the word 'Administration' while England uses the word 'Government' for the same thing.

The two words 'sick' and 'ill' mean broadly the same thing. But the English thought the Anglo-Saxon 'sick' too vulgar and frank and tended to give it up in favour of 'ill' of Scandinavian origin, considered more elegant on that account. The Americans, on the other hand, continued with the less formal 'sick', especially because it was hallowed by use in the Bible.

'Trade' now means to buy and sell, to do business. But originally it meant a tread, a path traversed, then a customary course of action, a recurring habit or manner of life. From this it acquired a restricted meaning, a business or work in which one engages regularly, a profession, a craft. Now though we still have this meaning in phrases like 'learning a trade', it has acquired the still more restricted meaning of commerce. Now a tradesman is one who sells commodities.

Words meaning the same thing but derived from different sources are retained not only because they could be adapted to showing different shades of meaning, but also because all kinds of motives and social factors enter into this development. There could be motives of pride or learning. Some expressions are considered genteel, others loud; some are considered too tame, others too suggestive; some too frank, others too prudish. So the words are accepted or rejected according to the prevailing scale of preference. In Great Britain of a hundred years ago, anatomical facts like 'leg' or 'belly' or 'breast' could not be mentioned in polite society especially in the presence of ladies. Now there is no such inhibition. In modern America and Europe, no word is frank enough, obscene enough.

In England, amongst the genteel, there is a tendency to use stomach rather than belly, domestic rather than servant, mirror rather than looking-glass, endeavour rather than try, assist rather than help, close rather than shut, proceed rather than go. H.W. Fowler has collected many such examples but they may have already gone out of date as a result of fast changes in the linguistic mores of England ever since he wrote.

A word is replaced by another under the impact of new ideas, theories and associations. For example, it has been suggested to replace a word like prostitution by behaviour-problem, alms by philanthropy or relief or rehabilitation or family welfare. Vice is habit-disease, sin psycho-neurosis, punishment treatment, penitentiary colony. Those who want to change their social status start by first changing their names. Barbers, undertakers, janitors now respectively call themselves beauticians, morticians, superintendents. H.L. Menken has given many such examples. In our own country, Gandhiji changed the name of the untouchables with a view of raising their social and ideological status. He called them *Harijans*, people of God. We now have toilets, retiring-rooms, washing-rooms—all euphemisms for words considered too direct or undisguised for a polite society.

Thus a word is not a mere referent. It must refer to a thing in a particular way. It has to respond to the ideas, ideologies and idiosyncracies of the age.

IV

These examples show how new objects and ideas are named. The process consists not in inventing brand-new names but in finding old ones that will cover new cases. In this way, old words are able to serve new needs, renew their life, and retain their sense of continuity. Through this process, we are also able to incorporate new experience and harmonize it with the old.

This is made possible because, in an important sense, the new is not so new; it is continuous with the old. New facts express old functions.

The process of naming probably involves, in a good many cases, sound-imitation. But it must be taking place at a very fundamental, nervous level; and it must be true only of primary and basic ideas, notions and situations. And also from the very start, or at least at a more recognizable level, a new principle which is not merely phonetic but is semantic must supervene.

For, let us remember that to imitate the sound of an object is not to name it. And even a name which expresses the nervous condition of a person in the face of an object is no true name. At best, an echoic name is a potential name. True name begins when it acquires a meaning beyond the object it names. To put it in another way, a true name consists not in what it refers to but in what it means, not in what it denotes but in what it connotes. It is an intellectual process, though the intellect works subliminally.

What happens is something like this. When we meet objects, we give them names after their most striking quality. In some cases, like that of many birds and animals, it may be their cry or sound. The crow, the pigeon, the partridge, the owl have received their names in this way. The crowing sound made by the 'crow' also earned it this name. The 'pigeon' derives its name from its cry of *pi, pi,* or at least what sounds like *pi, pi* to many of us. The 'partridge' derives its name from its noisy flight, its whirling wings. Some connect this sound with the Skt. *pard*, to break wind. The 'owl' (Skt. *ulūka*, L. *ulula*) owes this name to the hooting and howling cry it makes.

But their cry is not always the most striking feature of many birds and animals. Therefore, they derive their names from other traits. The 'horse' is named not from its neighing but from the swiftness of its movement. Many etymologists connect the word to L. *currere*, to run, which also gives us the word 'courser', another name for a horse. Similarly, a 'tiger' derives its name from the same trait, from the rapidity with which it attacks, and from its arrow-swift movement (Skt. *tigmas*, sharp, pointed;

modern Persian and also Hindustani *tīr*, an arrow). The Hindustani *cheetah*, belonging to the family of the lion, derives its name not from its roar but from spots on its body (Skt. *citra*, variegated). A wolf (Skt. *vṛka*) is 'the tearer' from the Skt. *vraśc*, to cut off or asunder. By some, a jackal (Skt. *śṛgāla*) is supposed to be 'the scavenger'.

Among the birds, the 'hawk' is probably so named because it pillages and plunders, the old meaning of *havoc*, probably of the same origin as *heave*, to lift, to seize. Similarly, the 'falcon', belonging to the same family as the hawk, derives its name from the hooked shape of its claws, or from its curved beak or wings (L. *falx*, a sickle, scythe, pruning-hook). The bird 'plover' arrives with the rainy season; it derives its name from this fact (L. *pluvia*, rain).

A 'wasp' probably derives its name from the fine nest it weaves for itself. As a wasp is a weaver, a 'spider' is a spinner; in Sanskrit, a spider is called *ūrṇa-vābhi*, wool weaver; *vābhi* in the compound word is from the root *vabh*, to weave, which became obsolete early in Sanskrit but which was still active in other Indo-Aryan languages and gave us the words 'web' and 'wasp'.

Thus we see that not all names are echoic in origin. But even if it is so, it is merely the first term in a complicated series. The first name of an object may be imitative, but in its turn it becomes the base of the names of other ideas which are hardly so. The cry *pi, pi,* for example, may give us the word pigeon, but pigeon becomes the base of new names. It characterizes new ideas in a nonechoic manner. This gives us words like 'pigeon-hearted', meaning timid, and 'pigeon-livered', meaning gentle and mild. It even gives us the word 'pigeon-hole', which through a process of meaning-transfer, connotes the idea of laying aside, classifying and categorizing. The word also expands in meaning. Passing through a curious route, it also acquired the meaning of 'an object of special concern', or 'business' in phrases like 'this is not my pigeon'. Pigeon is no longer a mere piper, it is also 'an easy target', 'a dupe'.

Similarly, the echoic 'crow' supports other tiers of meaning. It also means 'to gloat', 'to exult'. In phrases like 'as the crow flies', it means 'in a straight line'.

The echoic 'garg' and 'gurg' may give us the word 'gorge', meaning throat. 'Garg' probably also gives us 'jargon', a noise made in the throat, mere rhetoric. 'Gorge', in turn, gives us the French *gorgias*, a necktie. Probably this was considered too fine and showy and thus gave us the word 'gorgeous'. Others derive this word differently which will connect it with the word 'jargon'; 'gorgeous', they say, comes from the Greek rhetorician 'Gorgias' known for his ostentatious living and for his oratory.

Whether this particular derivation is correct or not, it is difficult to say. But a language does abound in names of general import which derive from names of individuals. Not only do we give to individuals names of larger significance, even names beyond their merit and moral and intellectual attainments but the names of individuals too become names of larger ideas and concepts. In English, we have many such examples in 'boycott', 'lynch', 'chauvinism', 'mercurial', 'venereal', 'guillotine', 'fabian', 'epicure', 'masochist', 'sadist', 'philander', 'spoonerism', 'solecism', 'pander', 'italics', 'braille', 'fahrenheit', 'laconic', 'gin', 'sherry', 'sandwich', 'tantalize', 'jingoism', and so on.

The semantic process is subtle and ubiquitous. It is both psychological as well as intellectual. It operates both in echoic as well as in non-echoic names. It will hold good even if the first names were conventional.

And, in a sense, all names are conventional. A child in the process of growth receives his vocabulary from his elders on authority. He does not participate in the psychological and intellectual process of creating the first language, the kind that we have been discussing. So, in this sense, his language—and by that token the language of all of us—is the language of convention and authority and consensus.

But it makes no difference. For even if the first name is received on authority, it soon begins to absorb the meaning of the referent and stand for like qualities in future. The fundamental semantic process now works through the conventional name, converting signs into symbols, investing them with new meanings, and making them capable of new applications.

The process of naming is complicated and deeply psychological. It operates at a subconscious level. Different elements that go into the making of a name—the referent, the sound, the meaning—all tend to coalesce in the mind so much so that it is difficult to separate them from one another. Ordinarily, the mind thinks like this: A mosquito is so named because it is so inconsequential; or an elephant is so named because it is so huge and majestic, realizing little that the elephant derives its name not from the hugeness of its body but from its ivory tusk. But even then, the mind's instinct is right. It intuits a semantic relationship between an elephant and its massiveness, its enormous size—ideas which are rendered by the word 'elephantine'.

We have seen that things derive their names from their attributes but it is possible that the attributes chosen are not the most characterisitic. In that case, names given will be inadequate.

The process of naming may also be too much forced or fanciful; it may not be in keeping with the deeper wisdom of the mind. Names thus derived may enjoy a measure of popularity for a time but are bound to disappear in due course. By the same token, names that reflect the deeper processes of the mind will have a longer life.

Alduous Huxley made a verb out of a proper noun from Gustave Flaubert's novel, *Madame Bovary*. Conceptualizing the life of the character depicted in the novel, he gave us the word 'to bovarise', meaning to believe that one is different from what one really is. The word gives a name to a very important trait of the mind but it failed to catch. Probably the coinage was too self-conscious. Or perhaps, there is more to the life of a word than its appropriateness. Perhaps, like individuals and nations, words too have their destiny, their luck, their allotted time, and even their ruling stars. Like every thing else, they are subject to the corroding influence of time. In due course, they lose their freshness and vitality.

Sometimes, certain names and thoughts go out of fashion because they do not agree with the ruling passion and ideology of the age. When the heart loses sympathy or the mind loses vision, words also lose their innerness and contract in meaning. Through a certain shift in the consciousness or in the gravity of life, even good and honourable words may become false—words of courtesy and consideration may become words of mere insincere politeness; words of righteousness may become words of self-righteousness; words may be used not to express but to conceal thought. They begin to ring false. They also become outer, superficial and frivolous, conveying only surface meanings. In short, they lose their innerness, authenticity and form. How can they be saved from this fate?

These are important aspects relating to the life of words. We shall discuss these questions in due course, but meanwhile, let us turn our glance and look at their more embryonic, radical forms and see what they have to teach us.

CHAPTER 3

Roots

From the examples we have given above, one thing stands out prominently: that words have histories. A word can always be traced back to a dim past, to its more ancestral forms.

The study of this aspect of words is called etymology. Etymology tries to trace back the history of a word to its earliest recorded form; it also tries to trace its transmission from one language to another. Further, it tries to formulate the laws of sound shifts in this process of transmission and historical changes.

This study reveals that words are often made up of several component parts; that of these parts not all are equally important but some constitute the very soul of these words. Most of the changes that occur in the chequered history of a word or in its pilgrimage from country to country and language to language revolve round this basic part. Etymology tries to identify these basic parts, tries to trace them and their cognates in other languages and to their ancestral forms. It studies root-words and cognate words; it studies etymons and morphemes and vocables that abide through various inflections and changes. It also studies these changes themselves, changes in phonetics and meanings as the words march down through the corridors of time in various disguises and trappings. It is found that these changes are not arbitrary; they follow a pattern.

It is interesting to follow words in their twists and turns and changing shades of meanings. It is interesting to see how through various inflections, vicissitudes, variations and changing forms, certain root-meanings and root-sounds remain relatively stable. Through apparently dissimilar words, one goes back to their ancestral forms from which they all are derived. This common parentage unites them in a new bond, a new family of relationships. A language is no longer a compendium of disparate, self-sufficient, arbitrary units called words. Words become parts of a family, brothers and sisters, cousins and in-laws.

A word also incarnates the history of a people. When the generations that speak a particular language die, words stay and their meanings stay with them. In fact, by the study of words and their successive meanings, it is possible to reconstruct the history of a race. It is like archaeology. Different meanings and shades of meanings stay embeded in different layers of a word, but one must learn to dig deeper and deeper into them and to be able to interpret the data properly to be able to find the hidden treasures there.

Suppose a people speaking a particular language get dispersed for one reason or another. In course of time, they are subject to different environments, stresses and strains and even lose the memory of their common ancestry. But in the deeper, unconscious part of their minds the words will preserve this memory and also embody the new experiences they have undergone.

We have also observed that a word is a living organism. Very often, a word is made up of several parts or limbs and, as in a human body, some parts are more essential than others. One part is prefixes and suffixes and infixes, just like hands and feet and other limbs in a human body. But a word has also its more vital parts where its life resides. It is called its stem, its root, its radical form, its core-sound. This radical root puts on many forms, enters into different combinations that modify its meanings beyond recognition. But the essential life resides there. It abides, persists through all ups and downs and disguises. Time may cover it with the moss of neglect, disuse and even abuse, but the essential meaning lies there like a smouldering coal covered over with ash. It could lie there dormant for generations but it again revives though often with changed meanings and in a disguised form under favourable circumstances. It dies and it rises again, Phoenix like, from its own ashes.

In the Sanskrit language, this sense of etymological unity, the sense of a mighty, luxuriant tree growing out of a limited number of root-syllables, is well preserved. The whole rich vocabulary of the Sanskrit language could be referred to 2,000 roots (1,750 distinct radical forms with 2,490 different meanings) which themselves are modifications of simpler elements.[1] Pāṇini gives a list of 2,343 roots excluding the Vedic roots which he omits. Of these only 500 are in use today. Some think that there are no more than 120 primitive roots.

These roots are generally monosyllabic, consisting of one consonant or two and combined with a vowel. Sometimes, the radical form is only a vowel. These forms are expanded by taking on affixes, suffixes and infixes. These again are expanded by the addition of prepositions, compounds, and compounds of compounds. This raises an edifice of half a million words.

We can see the same process at work in other inflectional languages like Persian, Greek and Latin. Another language which is very rich in this quality is Arabic. From a simple root of two or three consonants one could have hundreds of derivatives. For example, the root *ktb*, to write, gives *kitāb* (book), *kātib* (writer), *maktūb* (letter), *maktab* (office), *kutāb* (primary school), *maktabāḥ* (library), *kitābat* (writing), *mukātabat* (mutual correspondence), *kitābaḥ* (the name-plate on a building or grave), *katībaḥ* (army), etc. Another root *qtl*, to kill, gives *qātil* (killer), *maqtūl* (the one killed), *maqtal* (place where killing takes place), *quitāl* (killing, war), *muqātalaḥ* (mutual killing).The root *kvn* gives *makān* (house), *makīn* (dweller in a house), *ka-in* (the one who is born), *kaun* or *kā-ināt* (creation, world), *imkān* (possibility), *mumkin* (possible), *mutamakkin* (that which grasps a place, stable). The root *qvm* gives *maqām* (staying place), *qiyām* (stay), *qā-imaḥ* (post, pillar), *qā-im* (stable), *qaum* (nation), *qiyāmat* (day of judgement), *qaumaḥ* (the standing posture during Muslim worship), *qayyūm* (God, who always is), *qa-imaḥ* (angle of 90°), etc. Another root *qsd,* gives *qasd* (desire, resolve), *maqsid* (aim), *maqsūd* (desired, aim), *qāsid* (messenger), *iqtisād* (economy), *iqtisadīyāt* (Economics), etc.

---

[1]M. Monier-Williams, *Sanskrit-English Dictionary*, Introduction, p. xiii, fn. 5.

The Persian language is also inflectional in character. A root like *guftan*, to speak, gives *guftaḥ* (that which has been said), *guft* (saying), *guftagū* (mutual talk), *guftanī* (worth saying), *guftār* (speech, words), *goyāyi* (the power of speech), *goyā* (as if, speaker), etc. The root *raftan,* to go, gives *raftār* (gait, speed), *raftaḥ* (gone or dead), *raftaḥ raftaḥ* (slowly), *raftanī* (who is worth going, who is likely to go), etc.

Though English is a Germanic language, it is considerably Latin and French in its vocabulary language. Many of its words are inflectional in character, though this is not widely realized. For example, as in the Sanskrit language, from the verbal root *dā*, to give, we have *dāna* (giving), *adāna* (not giving), *pradāna* (gift), *abhidāna* (bestow for a purpose), *dātṛ* (giver), *dānīya* (worthy of gifts), *dātavya* (to be given), *dāya* (gift); similarly, in English we have from the same root words like donation, endowment, dowry and even anecdote, dose, condone, pardon, dative, and data. The line of transmission is through Greek and Latin. From the word 'give' of Anglo-Saxon origin, we have the words 'gift' and even 'forgive', and also 'gavel' (tribute), now out of use.

But English is tending to become, at least in its names, nomenclature and word-formations, an isolating type of language. Each word tends to stand apart. Their inter-connections and family relationships, their history and growth tend to be forgotten.

For example, an average English-knowing man may still see that prefixes and suffixes have gone into the making of such words as im-possible, il-legal, al-mighty, meta-physics, forth-coming, mis-take. But not many could guess that the following words are not one but combinations of words and prepositions: af-fair, l-ute, am-brosia, an-oint, ann-oy, anth-em, ba-lance, en-ergy, en-emy, de-luge, anci-ent i-gnore, belli-c-ose, apo-logy, sy-stem, e-normous, e-mit, oc-casion, meth-od, s-ample. And who will think that the word particle is not one word but contains two diminutives (cu and la)? The word is a compound one—parti-c-le, very, very small part.

Similarly, who could guess that there is a common root,

L. *pendēre,* to hang, allied to a still older Skt *spand,* to vibrate, in the following words: pend-ent, pend-ul-um, pens-ible, ap-pend, com-pendium, de-pend, ex-pend, im-pend, s-pend, sus-pend, sti-pend, per-pend or in pens-ion, pens-ive, com-pens-ate, dis-pense, ex-pense, pre-pense, pro-pense, also in poise, pansy, ponder, pound, pre-ponderate?

In the Greek and Latin languages also, like the Sanskrit, prepositions and affixes are attached to simple basic roots and words to yield compound words with modified meanings.

II

Now let us look more closely at these roots and see what they do to a language and how a whole edifice of vocabulary arises on their foundation. We need not go into the question whether, historically speaking, names and nouns come first or whether verbs come first. Verbs, nouns and adjectives are distinct only grammatically. In thought, they are one and melt into one another. It is enough for our purpose to note that when we study a language analytically, at the back of apparently most dissimilar words, we find a syllable, which persists through various changes in the outer structure of those words and which seems to bind them, if we reflect sufficiently, in a bond of unity. It is a kind of nucleus which we find at the heart of many word-forms. Let us illustrate this point with a few examples.

Let us take a Sanskrit root, *sthā*. Some of the modifications it undergoes are purely conjugational to indicate time and mood of the action in a sentence, but the root also goes into the making of such words as *sthala* (place, dry firm land, tableland), *sthāla* (receptacle, plate, cup), *sthāṇu* (stationary, firm), *sthāna* (place, position, posture), *sthāpatya* (architecture, building), *sthāvara* (immovable), *sthira* (firm, solid, compact), *sthita* (standing firm), *sthiti* (standing upright, position), *sthūṇa* (post, pillar), *sthavira* (strong, powerful, ancient, venerable, old), *sthūla* (stout, massive, thick, coarse). By adding certain prefixes to the root, we get another order of words with modified meanings like *adhi-sthā* (to dwell) *anu-sthā* (to perform), *ava-sthā* (to stand still), *vyava-sthā* (to remain), *ut-sthā* (to rise), *upa-sthā* (to wait upon), *ni-sthā* (to be versed in), *pra-sthā* (to set out).

We meet this word in other Indo-Aryan languages also, with a little change as a result of sound-shifting. In Greek, it is *histasthai*, to stand; in Latin *stāre*, to stand; in German *stehen*, to stand. Travelling through these routes, the original root enters into such present-day English words as stand, state, station, stationary, statue, status, stature, statuette, statuesque, stage, statute, stamina, stamen, statics, still, stead, steady, steadfast, stow, stall, apostasy, stable, statistics, standard, etc.

We find the same story repeated if we take other roots. The Sanskrit root *bhū* has given us hundreds of words like *bhava* (existence), *bhavana* (abode, mansion), *bhūti* (existence, might, prosperity), *bhūta* (what has been, creature, being) *bhaviṣya* imminent, future), *bhavya* (existing, likely to be, excellent, beautiful), *bhāva* (being, truth, state, condition, sentiment, disposition of the mind), *bhāvin* (future). Then the addition of certain prefixes to the root has given other words like *pra-bhu* (excelling, mighty, lord), *pra-bhāva* (might, power, majesty), *pra-bhava* (source, origin), *parā-bhava* (defeat, humiliation), *vi-bhū* (all-pervading), *vi-bhvan* (far-reaching, pervading), *vibhūman* (extension, greatness), *pari-bhava* (insult, disgrace, injury, contempt), *svayam-bhū* (self-born), *sam-bhava* (meeting occurrence, possibility), etc.

The Greek form of this root is *phynai* (to be born, be by nature) and *phyein* (to bring forth). It has given to the English language words like, physic, physics, physiology, physician, physiognomy, euphuism. The Latin form is *fui,* I have been. It has given the word future. From its Old High German form *būan*, to dwell, and Old English form *bēon*, to be, we derive words like build, bower, byre, booth, boor, busk, be.

Similarly, the Sanskrit root *jñā*, to know, has given us *jñāna* (knowledge), *jñāta* (known), *jñāti* (intimately acquainted, a near relation), *jñapti* (intelligence), and *ājñā* (permission), *anu-jñāna* (permission) *ava-jñā* (despisement), *abhi-jñā* (recognition), *prati-*

jñā (promise), *vi-jñāna* (ascertainment), *sam-jñāna* (unanimity, right conception).

In Greek, it appears in a reduplicated form in *gignoskein;* Latin form is *gnoscere* or *noscere*, to come to know; Old High German is *bichnāan*, to know, to recognize; Russian is *znate*. These have given to the English language knowledge, acknowledge, gnostic, ignorant, noble, cunning, keen, can, ken, narrate.

These examples could be easily multiplied but it is not necessary. It is enough for our purpose to feel the unity of words that apparently look dissimilar, to see that they are held together like beads on a thread. The thread is provided by the lowly and upretentious roots.

These examples do not yet show how primary, seed-syllables came to have the primary, seed-meanings they have. We do not know whether their mutual link is an arbitrary one—though there is no record of a body of men getting together to call certain ideas by certain syllables. We are personally inclined to believe that the relationship is natural and intimate, though it is difficult to explain it and to demonstrate it.

But once a particular sound or syllable has been chosen to stand for a particular seed-idea or action, the rest of the process is relatively clear though there must still remain important questions to answer. We can see the tree of language growing. We can see a seed-syllable raising a family of words. At first sight, the members may appear to be unrelated. For example, what is there in common between a statue, stall, statistics, and apostasy? Or between physics, build and bower? But if we keep the core-syllable and its meaning in mind, we can easily appreciate that the relationship between these words is a just one. They are linked in a common bond. They are held together by an inner appropriateness. Their referents invoke in the mind a common quality—though that is not the only quality they invoke. But this is a suggestion we shall take up later on. It is enough to note for the time being that words have strong psychological links.

There is another point which the above examples help to bring out in relief. A word is a living thing. It is pregnant with life and possibilities. It grows and expands and unfolds its meanings in a hundred directions. The process of unfoldment and development, like all truly vital processes, is unconscious but truly intelligent and wise. When you study the links between the words of the same family, you find them sensible ones.

Words are related because they develop a related sense of the basic idea. Dip, deep, dive, dove are illustrations in hand. Ride, rider, road, raid and perhaps even ready are other examples. A road, a rider, and a roadster are physically speaking different things but they are functionally related. This relationship is brought out by their common origin in a common root-syllable. Similarly, in Sanskrit, we have the words *ratha* (chariot), *rathin* (charioteer), *rathyā* (carriage, highway), illustrating the same principle. The other words are *patha* (road), *pathika* (traveller), *pathaka* (guide), *pātheya* (provision for a journey), *pathya* (suitable for journey, hence proper, wholesome diet).

Similary, the relationship between sit, seat, session, seance, sediment and residence can be easily appreciated; but other derivatives like sedentary, insidious, dissidence, subsidiary and obsession are also equally apt.

In Sanskrit, one word for a tree is *vṛkṣa*. Some derive it from the root *bṛh*, which means both to tear, pluck and also grow; others connect it with the root *vraśc*, to cut down, hew. In either case, the derivation is appropriate. A tree is that which grows or that which is felled.

Similarly, take the word 'rat'. It is related to and derived from the same source as words like erosion and corrosion. It is derived from the L. *rodere*, to gnaw. Behind this is probably the sense of the Skt. *rad*, to bite, scratch, which gives us the Skt. word *rada*, a tooth. Some etymologists believe that the words erase, abrase, and razor are also connected with the same origin.

Another name for a rat is *mūṣaka* or *mūṣika* or *mūṣa* in Sanskrit. It is derived from the verbal root *mūṣ*, to steal. This root also gives us the Gk. *mus*, L. *mūs*, Swedish *mus*, Rusian *muish*, Ger. *maus* and the English *mouse*. A mouse is a stealer.

Mouse has given us some other words like '*muscle*'. A muscle must have looked like a little mouse (L. *musculus*) to the name-givers.

III

A word does not merely develop the meaning of its root. Waiting in the memory bank or floating in a psychic matrix, its meanings are modified by association with other words of similar sound or import. For example, take the word 'surround'. Etymologically, it derives from L. *undāre*, to flow, or *unda*, a wave (Skt. *und* or *ud*, to flow, bathe, giving us *udan*, water; giving us other cognates like Gk. *hudōr,* Gothic *watō,* Lithuanian *wanduō*, Ger. *wasser*, all meaning English water). The L. *unda*, a wave, had the sense of 'overflowing', 'plentiful'. These two senses enter into all the words, like abundant, redundant, abound, surround, derived from *undāre.* But though 'overflowing' was the primary meaning of the word 'surround', its meaning has been modified by association with the word 'round' which indeed has quite a different derivation. As a result, now surround means to envelop, to encompass and not abound.

The meaning of a root-syllable is not a fixed quantity, clearly and mechanically marked and understood. The meaning is broad and protean and capable of many applications, as we have seen in the above examples. Sometimes a stem gives rise to words which develop its different potential meanings; sometimes one word has to make do and express the several meanings of its root.

For example, take the words 'satisfactory', 'sate' and 'satiate'. All the three are derived from the L. *sat*, *satis*, enough, *satur*, full; but while the 'enough' of a thing could 'satisfy' one, it could 'sate' another. So the same stem gives two words which express two possibilities of the mind. That which should satisfy could satiate if an inner culture is lacking. They also provide a commentary on our objects of desire or on our two experiences. One could say that that which satisfied also sated or that what we call our satisfaction is a form of satiation. When some people say they are satisfied, they are only sated.

The word 'sad' is also akin to the same source. Its equivalents

Gothic *sath*, Ger. *satt,* L. *satur*, all mean full, filled, sated, satisfied. Satiation makes for weariness and tiredness and eventual sadness. Or, there is a kind of filling and glutting which makes for heaviness, dullness and sorrowfulness. These are legitimate meanings, even when they appear to be opposed, which these words develop from the same stem.

These two senses, higher and lower, appear to be inherent in the meaning of any stem. For example, take another word, 'simple'. It is derived from the L. *simplex* which literally means one-fold, opposed to L. *duplex*, two-fold. The word means guileless, straight. In Sanskrit, it would mean *nirgrantha*, one without knots. But there is a kind of simplicity which lacks discrimination and borders on stupidity. So there is another word to convey that sense, 'simpleton' which means foolish, credulous or easily deceived.

Similarly, there is the word 'morose'. It derives from the L. *mōrōsus*, self-willed. In a good sense, it meant scrupulous; in a lower sense, it meant peevish. Now the lower sense has supplanted the good sense completely.

The word 'moral' like the word 'morose', derives from the same source, L. *mor* from *mos*, custom, will. 'Moral' means behaviour in conformity with the customs of the people or action done with a good-will. It now means ethical behaviour, while morose, from the same source, means someone sullen and gloomy. Good-will is necessary for good action; but if it is not good enough, it makes a man fastidious and difficult to please. So the two words seemingly so opposed are psychologically related. And because they are related, they are also sometimes confused. While virtue tends to make some people morose, others feel moral when they are only gloomy and sullen.

Of the two senses inherent in a stem, sometimes one age develops one sense, another age another sense. For example, take the word 'sullen'. It is derived from the L. *solus*, alone. And once it only meant that—solitary. But a later age brought out the other psychological implications of this way of life. Now it means one who hates company, who is gloomy, who is resentfully silent, who is angry.

Take another word 'silly'. The word once meant happy, blessed, innocent. But whether the thinking of the age changed or it was inherent in the original meaning, the meaning of the word has now changed beyond recognition. Silly now means pitiable, feeble, harmless, foolish. Innocence is innocuous; therefore, feeble. People also no longer seek the blessedness of happiness; they seek power and possession.

In any case, as is obvious from the above discussion, a word has generally to bear the burden of several meanings inherent in its stem. Sometimes one meaning is dropped and another is taken up, or one is in the background and another is in the forefront. But generally one word has several meanings piled up layer upon layer.

Take a few examples like 'cavalier', 'chivalrous', and 'gallant' to illustrate this point. The word 'cavalier' derives from L. *caballus*, a horse, and means a horseman. In its higher sense, it meant a gallant, chivalrous person. But it also means a debonair, one given to off-hand dismissal of men and matters, one with an aristocratic contempt for the common herd. A horseman, which at one time meant one belonging to the higher class, was capable of behaving in two opposite ways. And, therefore, the word expresses both these senses of the word.

The word 'chivalrous' too had the same two senses. It derives from Old French *cheval*, a horse, and meant a mounted man-at-arms. Then it came to describe his qualities of martial valour and knightly skill. Later on, it began to describe a mere social class of gallant or distinguished gentlemen. But to provide a higher ideal of conduct for this class, chivalry was also defined as valour, generosity, honour, courtesy, especially courtesy towards women. A word must describe the actual as well as the ideal status of an idea.

Again, take the word 'gallant'. It has passed through a whole gamut of meanings. Originally it meant gay, splendid, festive, ornate—the word 'gala' still retains that sense. It meant a young man of fashion, showy in dress or bearing; then attentive to ladies, or given to amorous intrigues, or just any civil person. The psychological links are clear. Over-dressed people show off their dresses and they put on manners as they put on ornate clothes for amorous purposes; their civility is a form of amorous game, amorous intrigue. Then from the sense of one who paid court to ladies and fought for them, it acquired the meaning of one who was courteous and brave.

All the words quoted have several layers of meaning, as we have seen.

IV

But there are other words of great moral import which exemplify almost perfectly the truth that words develop their inner meanings. The few examples given incorporate elements of historical experience, but there are words which in developing the original sense of the stem express those deeper moral truths which are in a sense ahistorical. For example, take the word 'virtue'. Its Sanskrit ancestor is *vīra*, manly or brave. Its immediate source is L. *uir*, man, or *uirtūs*, manly. Then it was extended to mean virtue in the present sense of 'excellence' and 'goodness'. It also acquired a third meaning—'effectual' or 'having effect' in phrases like 'by virtue of'. So the phrase means manliness, courage, merit, goodness, authority and power. A related Sanskrit word would perhaps be *pra-śasta* or *udāra* meaning noble, lofty, high, illustrious, great, best, generous, upright, liberal, gentle, effective, energetic, good, happy, and auspicious.

All these meanings are not joined by convention. They are joined and held together by a psychic force, by an inner nuclear pull, by an inner spiritual appropriateness. From the above example, it is clear that the meanings 'merit', 'excellence', and 'goodness', or at least an important part of these meanings, could only be expressed by a word which also means 'manliness'. These meanings represent a deep inner unity and the link between them is a *necessary* one, to use a philosophic term. So the bond between a word and its meaning is not conventional, artificial or contingent. The relationship comes into being through an inner spiritual process with an intuitive perception and hidden wisdom working at the back. The meanings of a word are inherent in it, some manifest, others still in seed-form: There is nothing artificial about them.

These meanings go together even when there are two different words in two different languages and drawn from two different roots. For example, take the word 'beauty'. It immediately derives from *beau*, which itself comes from L. *bellus*, handsome, fine, fair. But *bellus* itself is a specialized variant of *bonus*, good. *Bonus* in turn connects beauty to 'bounty' through *bonitas*. Some would also like to link them up with the Vedic *duvas*, honour, reverence, worship, gift. Thus the unconscious wisdom of the mind sees a connection between beauty, goodness and liberality. Or, at least there is a beauty in goodness which goes beyond prettiness; similarly, there is a comeliness which only comes from goodness and liberality. So the good is also the beautiful and the bountiful. It is also reverence and worship.

In Sanskrit, these related meanings are expressed by another word of a different origin—*śrí*. The word means light, lustre, glory, beauty, prosperity, dignity, auspiciousness, success, riches, majesty. In the intuitive vision of the soul, these qualities go together. There is beauty and glory in light and with them go prosperity, auspiciousness, and majesty.

Take another English word 'glad'. It now ordinarily means cheerful, happy; but it has other shades of meaning also. Its older Anglo-Saxon meaning was shining, bright. Its old Germanic form '*glatt*' also meant smooth, even. Through a Scandinavian channel, it is also related to '*glade*' which means an open space in a wood. The mind has perceived a link between joy, light and space. The Upanishads say: 'There is a joy in the Vast'! To the logical positivists, these links are unfortunate and signify slovenly thinking but these are the very soul of a word, as we shall see more fully.

In Sanskrit, we have a similar word related to the above, related not etymologically but psychologically. The word is *prasanna* or *prasāda*, both derived from a root *pra-sad*. *Pra-sad* means to sit down, to settle down, to grow clear and bright, to become satisfied. The word provides not only interesting psychological links between different concepts but describes a whole system of Yoga. Sit down restfully; that will lead to tranquility; tranquility will lead to clarity and purity; purity will lead to joy.[2] These steps have been taught by Patañjali and the Buddha very clearly and analytically. Here a single word has preserved those teachings in a congealed form.

In these concepts, the flow from one meaning to another is fairly obvious. But there are words, particularly in the still higher realm, which unite even two opposite concepts.

For example, among the Hindus the word '*śiva*', the auspicious one, is also applied to *rudra*, the terrible one. In fact, Śiva and Rudra are two names of the same God. Amongst Greeks, the Furies were called *eumenides*, the gracious ones or benevolent ones or those of good will. Similarly, the night was called *euphrone*, benevolent.

V

We have discussed so far the development of words. We have seen how words develop from root-syllables and branch off into several pathways. We have seen how in their development while incorporating new historical experience they develop the seed-meanings of the seed-syllables. We have seen how words in their developed forms convey several meanings which sometimes appear wide apart but which, on a closer look, are found to be held together by an inner psychological affinity. There is no doubt that a stem could develop in hundreds of directions, but a language develops only some of its possibilities, just as it utilizes only a few dozen speech-sounds out of innumerable ones. One language develops one possibility; another language develops another. A

---

[2]'Light dawns for the righteous and joy for the upright in heart.' Old Testament, Psalms, 97.11.

possibility developed by one language could be dropped altogether by a sister language and it may branch off in quite a different direction. It may create a new word of its own or give old words new meanings and shades of meaning under the stress of new experiences. Words in one language may lose the memory of their ancestry, while this memory may be retained by words in some sister language. All these factors—sound-shifts, developments of seed-syllables in different directions, changed meanings under new circumstances, forgetfulness of original forms—contribute in making a new language out of an old one.

These new languages may develop the possibilities of a nucleus-syllable in their own diverse ways, but most possibilities still remain untapped. They remain latent. They are the source of future developments of a language. So, in a sense, seed-roots hold within themselves all languages, all meanings, actual and potential, past, present and future.

Can we enter into this larger life of words? Is it possible to establish some kind of contact with their hidden meanings? We shall have occasion to refer to these questions again.

CHAPTER 4

Synonyms

We started by raising the problem whether a name is a mere label or it expresses in some way the truth of its object. If a name was meaningful, we tried to find out in what sense, and how it was so. We discussed the nature of sound—the material out of which a name is fashioned—to determine whether the secret of its meaning lay there. This discussion led us to postulate the existence of sounds at a deeper and more subtle level than the one we ordinarily know in their more obvious spoken and audible aspects. A suggestion was made and discussed that it was perhaps at this subtle level that the sound of a word expressed the truth of the object it named.

The suggestion was interesting and probably in some sense true, but it had one great disadvantage—it was not sufficiently empirical.

Then we began studying the history and the process of name-giving. We found that the process consisted in this: that whenever there was a new thing to be named, an old word which was functionally related to it was found to designate it. In this way, we saw that most of the names were just and they expressed in some way the attributes of the things they named.

The study of the history of words led us to the study of the roots in which their root-meanings reside. This again proved to be a rewarding line of investigation. We saw a whole edifice of vocabulary rising on the foundation of a thousand or two thousand seed-words. We saw that one single root-word gave rise to a hundred related words; that there was nothing arbitrary in the birth of those words. Those words developed the multiple meanings inherent in the seed-word.

These discussions have been useful and they explain the majority of words in a language. We can see more clearly than ever before that these words are meaningful; that these meanings have not been tacked on to them arbitrarily. On the other hand, as these words unfold themselves, they express the nature and attributes of their objects and bring out their mutual relationships.

The foregoing discussions have yielded good answers, as we have observed. Yet do they really answer all the questions? In any case, can we not attack the problem from a fresh angle to strengthen the above conclusions and to remove certain lacunae?

For example, what is the answer to the question which can certainly be asked: if the word 'dog' is good enough for the English, 'cane' for the Italians, 'perro' for the Spaniards, 'hund' for the Germans, 'sobaka' for the Russians, then in what sense are these words more than labels for a particular object if that object could be indicated equally well by words as different as the above in sound? Will it be a satisfactory answer to say that all these words embodying different speech-sounds express the same subtle sound which conveys in some way the meaning of the same object—dog? The question is just and we shall now try to answer it as best we can.

II

Any object invokes more than one suggestion and conveys more than one idea. Therefore, it calls for more than one name to describe it. No object is simple enough to convey only one idea to be designated by only one root-word. Therefore, generally a language has several words to describe several ideas suggested by the same object. Also, one language may develop one suggestion; another language may develop another suggestion. That may account for different words in different languages and for several words in the same language.

For example, a river evokes many images. As a result, it has many names. Because it moves and goes downwards, in Sanskrit it is called *āpagā* and *nimnagā*; it goes down to join a sea, therefore it is called *samudragā* and *sāgaragāminī*; it has banks, therefore it is called *taṭinī*; it is full of waves and billows, therefore it is called *taraṅgiṇī*. These names are somewhat poetic but the most commonly used names are *nada*, *nadī, sindhu*, *sarit* and *srotas*. The idea of the roaring sound that a river makes gives us the first two names, *nada* and *nadī*, from a Skt. root *nad*, to thunder, to roar, to cry. The word *sindhu* is from the root *sidh*, to go, and develops the idea of the movement of a river. Later on, it also came to be identified with a particular river, Sindhu of the Punjab.

In English, the fact that a river hews away its path is designated by the word 'river', derived from the verb *rive,* to split, tear; but it has no name for a river which develops the suggestion of a 'roaring noise'. The suggestion of 'flowing' is contained in the word 'stream', derived from the Gk. *rhein*, to flow; this itself has its ancestral form in Skt. *sru*, to flow, which gives us the word *srotas* in Sanskrit. Old English had a word 'flod', meaning a flowing stream, and especially a stream in spate; but now its modern form 'flood' only means 'inundation', meaning about the same thing as Skt. *plāvana*, derived from the root *plu*, to float, to swim; but *plu* itself is the base of two other English words, float and fleet.

Besides 'river', the verb 'rive' also gives us the words 'rift' and rifle'; 'rift' means to cleave, divide; and 'rifle' means to tear by rubbing, to plunder. Similarly, the root *sru* gives us both 'stream', as we have already seen, and also 'rhythm', harmonious movement. According to certain authorities, it also gives us the words 'rheum', discharge from the lungs or nostrils, 'catarrh', inflammation of or fluid discharge from the mucous membrane, and 'diarrhoea', loose bowels. So while etymologically speaking, 'river' belongs to the family of 'rift' and 'rifle'; and 'stream' to that of 'rhythm', 'catarrh', 'rheum' and 'diarrhoea'; in meanings they belong to another family sharing membership with other words like *nada* and *sarita*.

Similarly, the words 'bank' and 'shore' mean the same thing, but they develop two different suggestions of their common referent. 'Shore' derives from the Old English *scieran*, to cut, itself derived from L. *curtus*, shortened, and Gk. *keirein*, to cut or shear. So the original sense of the word 'shore' is a part shorn off or an edge. On the other hand, the word 'bank' means a ridge, an eminence, a mound of earth. Its older forms are Icelandic *bakki*, Danish *bakke* and Swedish *backe*. The same source gives us the words 'bench', 'table', (hence a merchant's counter and hence the modern 'bank') and 'banquet', the festive board.

Similarly, the words 'grass' and 'hay' refer to the same thing but are adapted to two different uses. They develop two different suggestions of the same referent. 'Grass' refers to that which grows (from Old English *grōwan*, to grow); 'hay' to that which is hewed (from Old English *heawan*, to hew). Sanskrit too has several words for this referent, embodying its various suggestions and adapted to different uses. Some of these names are—*ghāsa*, pasture grass, from the verbal root *ghas*, to consume or to devour; *tṛṇa*, blade of grass or straw grass, from the root *tṛṇ*, to eat; *śāda*, young grass, from *śad*, to hew or cut; *kuśa*, a particular grass with long pointed stalks once used in religious ceremonies, from the root *kuś*, to enfold; *darbha* (English 'turf'), a particular kind of grass, from the root *dṛbh*, to twine, to tie or string together; and *barhis* (Avestan *baresman*), a particular grass used at sacrificial ceremonies in old Vedic times, derived from the root *bṛh*, to pluck out.

We shall dwell on this point a little longer, partly because it provides a new bond of unity between the words of a language; and partly because it is characteristic of a consciousness which is developed in any degree beyond the material and the utilitarian to see more than one quality in an object and to give it names after those qualities. This trait is the very life-breath of a creative consciousness, particularly of a spiritual one, as we shall see more fully later on.

Let us take a few ordinary objects like fire and water and see what kind of names they have given birth to in some of the languages of the Indo-European family. To anticipate, we may point to certain interesting facts which such a study reveals.

We find that in the beginning different suggestions underlying a common object develop into different names, but in course of time these suggestions may be completely forgotten and the names may remain as pure designations. In fact, this is the fate of most of the names. In due course, they lose consciousness, lose psychological affinity with what they stand for. They degenerate from the significant to the conventional, from the connotative to the denotative, from the unique to the commonplace. No wonder that such names look like labels because they no longer tell us anything about their objects; they merely indicate them. They are mere tags.

One notices another interesting fact. A particular object gives rise to a particular name through a particular suggestion. Now one language of the Indo-European family may retain that name; another may give it up altogether but retain its root-suggestion in another name of similar import, that is, in the names of the ideas related to that object. The meaning will become clear as we proceed with our illustrations.

Now, for example, let us take the object indicated by the word 'fire'. It appears to be a simple object of observation which could do with one syllable or word to indicate it. Instead, it evokes multiple ideas, suggestions and emotions. It glows; it shines; it blazes; it heats; it cooks; it warms; it burns; it leaps up; it emits smoke; it gives a cozy feeling; people foregather round it on wintry nights. Different languages have evolved different names to bring out these different qualities, emotions and ideas. Indeed, in the same language, there are generally many names to indicate fire's different qualities. In Sanskrit, it has many names. It is called *anala* (from root *an*, to breathe) because it is endowed with the breath of life; *agni* (from root *ag*, to move tortuously) because it moves up windingly; *arciṣmat* because it is resplendent; *tejas* because it has a flaming glow (from *tij*, sharp); *samiddha* because it feeds on fuel; because it is fanned by wind, it is called *vāyu-sakhā,* having wind for a friend; because it moves along a smoky path, it is called *kṛṣṇādhvan* or *kṛṣṇavartman.*

The physical qualities become psychic attributes and spiritual attributes. *Arciṣmat* does not merely mean resplendent; it becomes the name of one of the ten stages through which a Bodhisattva must pass before becoming a Buddha. Fire is *vahni* (from root *vah*, to carry), bearer of oblations to Gods and Manes. She is also the partaker of those oblations, *huta-bhuj*.

The English word 'fire' is derived originally from a Sanskrit root *pū*, to purify. In Sanskrit, the root has given us the word *pāvaka,* that which purifies, another name for fire. Other languages lost the original sense but retained, in a modified form, the word based on that sense. The Greek word was *pyr*, German *feuer*, Danish and Swedish *fyr*.

The object called 'fire' conveyed not only the idea of purity but also of burning. The root *pū* gave us the words 'pure' and 'fire'; 'fire' in its turn gave us the word 'fiery'. The three words appear to be so different and yet they are suggested by the same object.

Some of the other ideas which the object called 'fire' suggests are those of blazing, flashing, singeing, glowing, shining, a conflagration. All these different ideas have given us words for fire though all languages have not developed these senses equally. These ideas are physical and basic and are found in all the languages; but psychological ideas based on them are differently treated in different languages and at different times. The fire of love is less consuming today than it used to be in more romantic days. Some important psychic and spiritual meanings of the word are going out of fashion these days and are not even understood by the modern mind.

Turning to the more physical meanings and examples, the word 'conflagration' is a name for a particular kind of fire. It is derived from L. *con* or *cum*, wholly, and *flagrāre*, to burn. So the word means 'great burning'. Latin *flagrāre* has its close kin in Skt. *bhrāj*, to shine brightly; and the root has given us not only the word conflagration but, at a second remove, also the words flagrant and refulgent.

The word 'singe' refers to the hissing and singing quality of a burning piece of wood. It now means to burn superficially and lightly. It has also not given rise to any substantive.

Fire warms. We have that sense in the English word 'thermal', which is derived from the Gk. *thermos*, hot, or L. *formus*, warm, hot. Some also derive it ultimately from the Sanskrit word *gharma*, heat, warmth. The word 'furnace' is also derived from the same source.

Fire shines. This sense is indicated by the Sanskrit root *cand* or *scand*, to shine or be bright, and L. *candēre*, to shine. This has given us not only the words candle, incense, and incendiary, but also the words candour and candid. Candid originally meant white, fair, sincere; then by an easy, psychological transition, it meant upright, frank, and open.

The word 'candidate' also derives from the same source. Latin *candidātus* meant white-robed. It refers to a custom among the Romans that a candidate for an office wore white robes.

The idea of heat suggested by fire has given its own group of words. In English, these words are calory, caldron, cauldron, calefaction. They are derived from L. *calēre*, to be hot, which also gave *caldāria*, a hot bath.

In English, there are not many names for fire, as there are in Sanskrit; but still certain roots which give different names of fire in Sanskrit also enter into certain English words which contain some of the suggestions conveyed by fire. For example, one word for fire is *samiddha*. It is derived from a verbal root *indh*, to kindle, which gives the word *edhas*, fuel. In English, this root is probably also related to the word 'oast', a burning heat, and the word 'oast-house', a kiln for drying hops. Even the words 'ether', 'estuary' and 'edifice' are derived, through Greek and Latin channels, from the same source. 'Ether' is from Gk. *aithein*, to ignite, blaze. Perhaps to the Greeks, the sky suggested the idea of blazing and glowing as to the Hindus it suggested the idea of shine or brilliance. Therefore, the Hindus had a word for it, *ākāśa*, from a root *kāś,* to shine, to be brilliant.

'Edifice' is from L. *aedes*, a house, a temple, a fire-place, a hearth. An edifice was perhaps a temple or a public place where fire was worshipped and perhaps also a little corner of the house where fire was kept for comfort or worship. It was perhaps because of this association with worship, temple and fire that the word 'edify' came to mean 'to instruct and improve spiritually'.

'Estuary' means a water passage where the tide meets a river current; especially, an arm of the sea at the lower end of a river. The word derives from L. *aestus*, boiling, tide; and is also akin to L. *aestas*, summer; both with their ancestor in Skt. *indh*, to kindle. When a river current meets the sea tide, heat or warmth is generated. Perhaps, the word estuary came out of that suggestion.

In Sanskrit, we have another word for fire, *anala,* derived from the root *an*, to breathe. To the Hindus, fire was a living, breathing person. In English, we do not have a name for fire derived from that root. But we have the same root in words like animal and animus. So there is life in fire and fire in life.

Sanskrit has another word, *agni*, the most common name for fire. Its Lithunian equivalent is *ugnis*, and in Slav it is *ogni*. In English, this gives indirectly the word *ignition* derived from L. *ignis*. *Ingle*, which is the Celtic name for fire, is no longer used.

But if *agni* derives from the root *aj*, to stimulate, to drive, to urge, as some etymologists suggest, then this root-suggestion enters into words like ache, agony, agent, agile. Who could imagine without a good deal of reflection that these words contain ideas and images suggested by fire?

To take another illustration, let us think of the object, common but important, denoted by the word 'water'. In Sanskrit, there are many words for it like *vāri*, *jala*, *udaka*, *toyam*, *āpa*, *nīra*, *ambhas*, *pānīyam*. Here, also, we meet the same phenomenon. The words must have come from diverse suggestions and developed different ideas suggested by water or its different forms. One language developed one sense, another dropped it altogether. One language formed a word to develop a particular suggestion of the object, another language borrowed it as a mere designation to indicate that object in a general way. One language used one sense indiscriminately to suggest another; while another language used it for a more specialized sense of water.

For example, the Sanskrit word *vār* or *vāri* means water, also giving us the word *varṣā*, rain. *Vāri* still means water in Sanskrit as it did long ago. But in English, it retains that connected sense only in a disguised form as in the word 'urine', itself derived from the L. *ūrīna* and Gk. *ouron*. The Anglo-Saxon word is *waer*, meaning the sea. The Icelandic words are *ūr*, drizzling rain, and *ver*, the sea. So we see how the senses change while the broad meaning remains the same.

Another word in Sanskrit is *āpas* or *ap*. According to some scholars, it is related to L. *aqua*, water, Gothic *ahva*, a stream, and Lithuanian *uppe*, a river.

Another Sanskrit word *ambhas* means water or rather celestial water. Its Greek version is *ombros*, a storm of rain, a thunderstorm sent by Zeus. It is distinguished both from drizzling rain as well as from a heavy but short-lived shower. The Latin word for *ambhas* and *ombros* is *imber*, heavy rain. It is distinguished from ordinary rain, *pluuia*, itself akin to *Skt. plu*, to float, swim, and Gk. *plunō*, I wash.

The Sanskrit word *udaka* is derived from a root *und* or *ud*, to flow out, to wet to bathe. It is akin to English *water*, Swedish *vatten,* Old Norse *vatn*, Russian *voda* and *vodka* (water and little water), Gk. *hudōr* and L. *unds,* all meaning water.

III

Now, after this little detour, we can go back to the word 'dog' again. Perhaps, we can now appreciate better why the object dog has different names in different languages and several names in the same language. The origin of the word dog itself is forgotten, though it itself has given birth to another word doggedness, meaning tenacity and obstinacy, qualities suggested by a dog. Sanskrit has many names for a dog—*śvā*, *śunaka*, *bhaṣaka*, *kṛtjña*, *śīghracetana*, *ratri-jāgara*, *śavakāmya*, *vakra-puccha*, *kukkura*, etc. Some of these names are merely poetic or learned, but others have a wider currency. *Śunaka* was originally a young dog, now any dog.

Latin *canis* meant a dog, and it had a particular reference to the family (*canidae*) which included dogs, wolves, jackals and foxes. It has given to the English language such words as canine, kennel, and even cynic and cynosure.

Latin *canis* is a variation of the Sanskrit *śvan.* It has its immediate predecessor in Gk. *kuōn*, and successor in Italian *cane*. Its Germanic form is *hund*, which gives us the English hound.

The Sanskrit *bhaṣaka* is an imitative word. It means a barker, a howler. In English, the word of imitative origin is *cur,* a 'growler', from Medieval English *curren*, to growl.

'Mongrel' has a double diminutive *mong-er-el* and originally meant a small puppy of mingled breed. A mastiff originally meant a tame, domestic dog, from L. *masuescere*, to tame, to accustom to the hand, or to domesticate.

So we see that originally, at least, different names were meant to develop different senses of a thing. It is only later that these distinctions were lost in the passage of time. In due course, some of these names became general and interchangeable designations for a dog.

This may account for different words for the same thing in different languages and for many names for the same thing in the same language.

IV

While we are about this subject, we may also discuss another related point. Not only does an object invoke several very different suggestions and ideas but the same idea could be evoked by widely different objects, experiences, and situations.

For example, the words menace, danger, threat, hazard, risk, peril mean about the same thing though they have also their individual nuances and a good writer will not find them always interchangeable. But they have been invoked by very different situations. '*Menace*' is from a L. verb *ēminēre*, to jut out, project. It gave the L. *minae*, things projecting, hence threatening to fall, and from that the meaning of threat.

'Danger' is from L. *dominus*, master; this gave us Old French *dangier*, a lord's jurisdiction, power. 'Dangerous' in Medieval English meant 'haughty' (like a master) and hence difficult and likely to inflict injury.

The word 'threat' has its ancestral Anglo-Saxon form in *thrēat*, a crowd, a throng of people, overcrowding. From this developed the meaning of a great pressure, calamity, trouble. Long before the present bursting cities, traffic jams, and exploding population, the human mind had seen trouble in a crowd and too many men.

The original meaning of the word 'hazard' was a game of chance played with dice from an Arabic word *al-zahr*, the die; this gave us the Spanish word *azar*, unlucky throw (at cards, etc.), unforeseen disaster. So the gambling board gave us the word 'hazard' with its present meaning of risk.

But the word 'risk' itself was suggested by a very different kind of situation. The present word comes from Italian *risico*, hazard, peril; but according to some scholars, this Italian word is the same as the Spanish *risco*, a steep abrupt rock, of possible danger to the sailors. Hence the present meaning of the word.

The word 'peril' derives from L. *perīculum*, an attempt; this in turn is akin to Gk. *peira*, a trial or attempt, and hence a risk, danger.

So we see that while the objects and situations are widely different—architectural, political, populational, nautical—the experience is similar and the idea invoked is the same. This provides a new point of unity between different objects on the one hand and their names on the other.

This point could be further illustrated. In the words 'coward', 'pusillanimous', 'effeminate', 'timid', 'timorous', the broad meaning is the same but the situations that invoked it are different.

The word 'coward' was suggested by the figure of an animal that dropped its tail. The word is made up of an Old French word *coe*, tail (Italian *coda)* and a suffix *ard*. So it means a person who turns or shows his tail and hence a man without courage.

'Pusillanimous' derives from L. *pusillus*, very small, and L. *animus*, mind, soul. *Pusillus* is also allied to *pusus*, a little boy, or *puer*, a boy (from which we also get the word 'puerile'). So pusillanimous is a person who behaves like a small mind, meanly or like a small boy. From this arose the meaning of lack of courage or resolution or the meaning of contemptible timidity.

'Effeminate' means womanish or weak. It derives from L. *fēmina*, a woman. So an effeminate person is one who is like a woman, weak.[1]

The two other words 'timid' and 'timorous', belonging to this group, derive from the L. *timēre*, to fear. According to some scholars, the Latin verb is allied to the Skt. *tam*, a gasp for breath, choke, faint.

Words like 'heavy', 'weighty', and 'ponderous' illustrate the same principle. They have a similarity of meaning though they come from different experiences. 'Heavy' is that which is hard to heave, that is, to raise and lift. 'Weighty' is from an Old English word *wegan,* meaning hard to carry; this word is akin to L. *uehere*, to carry or transport, and even to the still older Skt. *vah*, to move, carry 'Ponderous', meaning weighty, unwieldy, is derived from L. *ponderāre*, to weigh; this gives us the word 'pound', a weight-measure. So the idea of 'heaviness' derives from different experiences that involve lifting or transporting or weighing.

Similarly, with the words 'courage' and 'valour'. 'Courage' is suggested by a certain quality of the heart (from L. *cor*, Gk. *kardia*, both meaning heart). The ideas of strength, worth, dominion and sovereignty give us the word 'valour'.

The idea of light could be suggested equally well by the sun, the moon, the stars, lightning, dawn. The idea of grace could be suggested by any act of generosity, courage, faith or self-giving, by the smile of trust in the face of a child. The idea of the transitoriness of things could be suggested by a bubble, a comet,

[1]Whether weakness belongs to a woman or belongs to the ego of man is another matter and is a question that belongs to philosophy. But as a matter of historical record women have been considered weak in some sense by women as well as by men. Perhaps the best way of looking at the problem is that while there is nothing wrong in a womanly woman, the same cannot be said of a womanly man. There is also the fact that a certain kind of weakness is not always a great deprivation. A certain kind of muscular weakness in a child or a woman is even endearing and it has some higher function to fulfil in nature. In Sanskrit literature, a woman is called *bhīru,* the timid one, and it is an endearing mode of address.

a flake of snow, a may-fly, by the span of man's life or the measure of his happiness.

V

Thus we see that man could derive the same experience from widely different objects and situations. Outside objects could vary but the corresponding basic experience could remain the same. This fact has important implications and raises certain fundamental issues of philosophy, sociology and pedagogy. For example, the question can be raised whether these common qualities of experience belong to things or thought; whether thought and the objects of thought are really as exclusive and separate as we take them to be. Probably, they have many points of contact, a good deal of inner unity, and they share many common qualities and attributes.

Another implication is that a particular language is not the mere product of a particular environment, or economic system or social culture. For widely different objects, cultures and social and economic environments could give basically the same concepts and values, experientially speaking. This also means that nations and races that belong to different social systems, different levels of culture, different environments, are not necessarily different in their basic life-experience.

This thought runs counter to the dominant environmentalist thinking of the age. If widely different objects invoke the same experience, it means they do not have the primacy that we ordinarily give them. By changing the physical environment, you do not change its meaning. Different kinds of goods and services or different industrial and commercial environments do not change man's essential experience of them. Children learn and draw as much pleasure from cheap toys as from expensive ones—in fact, expensive toys are more for the satisfaction of the parents than for that of the children.

But it does not mean that the outside objects are dead or dumb. They are dumb to the extent a man is deaf. But to a person of deepened sensibility, they speak thoughts which others do not hear and reveal truths which others do not see. To the ordinary eye, the sky, the moon, the sun, fire, wind are ordinary physical phenomena; but to a heart that knows how to watch and receive in wise passiveness, they are full of a different kind of eloquence and message; to this heart, they are images of That. But of this aspect of the problem later on. Here, it is sufficient to observe that many objects though apparently dissimilar and many names of different etymological origins yet meet in experiential unity.

CHAPTER 5

Multiple Levels of Meanings and Their Underlying Unity

A word has multiple meanings. These it derives through various channels and in many ways. In the last chapter, we saw that one object invokes several suggestions and that a single suggestion is invoked by more than one object or situation. This fact provides words with new points of contacts and binds them in a new set of relationships.

The meanings of a word also exist in different layers and different modes. One of these layers—the very first, in one sense—consists of physical and sensuous meanings, supporting a secondary and even a tertiary layer of meanings more psychological and intellectual in character.

This is not a happy way though of putting our thought, for it suggests that the physical meanings are basic and the psychological and the intellectual meanings are derivatives. It is far from our intention to suggest this. The physical meanings may be primary meanings from a certain viewpoint and for certain purposes, but the order of primacy can easily change with the change in perspective, procedure and purpose. More often than not, we find that in real life, meanings of a word co-exist and interpenetrate. But for a fruitful discussion, we have to separate them in thought even when they are inseparable in fact. With this clarification in mind, let us now turn to our new discussion.

Words like burning, heating, and shining have certain physical qualities which it is easy to identify with fire. But they, in turn, enter into psychological and moral ideas like energy, eagerness, vigour, ardour, passion, inspiration, anger, violence, destruction, enthusiasm, excitement. Therefore, through them, fire suggests phrases like 'fire and sword', 'between two fires', 'go through fire', and such other phrases which stand for larger human situations and concepts.

Similarly, water suggests the more physical ideas of moistening, sprinkling, soaking, drinking; it also refers to concrete things like a stream, an ocean, rains, clouds. But it also soon begins to stand for man's other situations. In phrases like 'make one's mouth water', 'keep one's head above water', 'throw cold water on', 'cast one's bread upon the waters', it does more than describe an object called water. Water can stand for ocean but ocean can stand for an unsurmountable obstacle, something that divides and, with better communications, also something that unites. It can stand for unplumbed depths; in fact, one of its names is the deep, the abyss. It can suggest the idea of infinity, of interminableness, of vastness—all important components of a religious consciousness. And looking at the variety of living things inhabiting the seas and the lakes, and finding that man is mostly water, it can also stand for the principle of life, for immortality.

In fact, there is no object, however lowly, which does not yield a larger sense. The word 'stone' denotes not merely a mineral substance but it also stands for ideas and qualities of inflexibility, obduracy, insensitivity, pitilessness, and unresponsiveness. The simple object like earth or soil, denoted by the Latin word *humus*, gives us such larger ideas as homo, man (the earthly-one), humanity, homage, humiliate, and humble. 'Flower' and 'fruit' do not stand for physical things or physical processes only. A flower is not merely a shoot or a blossom; it is also the best, the finest and the most delicate part of any thing; it also stands for the idea of development and flourishing. Similarly, a fruit is not merely a succulent part or product of a plant; it also conveys the idea of progeny and offspring; it also means consequences, results, reward and punishment for all that one has thought and done.

There are two school of thought. One school says that flowers and fruits are merely names for certain physical facts and that their other non-sensuous meanings are merely extensions of their primary physical meanings. Another school says that they are really names for larger ideas and concepts which are of a general import and are intellectual and moral in essence; physical facts merely exemplify them on a physical plane. Which come first—physical referents or larger conceptions?

We shall not go into this question at this stage but merely note here that the physical, the psychological, and the spiritual are intimately related. A word exists simultaneously at several levels, the physical, the psychological, the moral, the spiritual. It is a meeting-point of all of them. Everything that we see and name has a larger meaning. Everything, however inconsequential, every animal, small or big, every odd and end, every pot and pin, point to truth beyond its bare physical meaning. Animals illustrate human life and men illustrate animal life.

Look at the following phrases and the point becomes clear. 'Eagles do not breed doves'; 'the raven does not hatch a lark'—two widely different kinds of animals but expressing the same truth; 'eagles fly alone while crows and starlings flock together'; 'what could you expect from a hog but a grunt'; 'the fox's viles will not enter the lion's head'; 'a fox should not be the jury at a goose's trial'; 'when the fox preaches, then beware of your geese'; in all these examples, animals convey truths beyond their physical meanings. In fact, every creature however humble—a fly, a flee, a fowl, a fish—is capable of conveying a larger truth.

The same is true of the non-animal world: 'empty vessels make much noise'; 'great shoes fit not a little foot': 'a great city, a great solitude'; 'fight with shadows'; in all these examples, referents prove truths beyond themselves. In fact, these truths can be expressed in other ways also, by other figures of speech, by naming other referents.

II

Certain conclusions follow. The utility of words as referents is limited and constitutes a small part of their life and purpose. In that role, they are lifeless. And if that were their only role, they would be saying precious little and would soon be emptied of life. But when they are released from their too physical confines, their imprisoned life is freed and they acquire movement and wings; they live.

As referents to physical things, words are separate, inert, dumb. But as they rise from mere physical status and acquire a more psychological existence, they begin to speak and tell a worthwhile story. But the tethering of a word to a physical fact need not take away anything from its power, beauty and independence. On the other hand, this association has its own reward. It lends to the words a certain discipline, a certain sensuous quality which they would otherwise lack and saves them from arbitrariness and abstraction. It also does not impair their pliability; you can still use them with understanding and responsibility but not unlawfully, uncontrollably, haphazardly; you cannot run amok with them.

It also makes these words fit for poetry. It helps them to express in the language of the senses what is beyond the senses.

Poets take advantage of this quality of words. They use one level of experience to suggest another. They use figures of speech, figures of comparison and contrasts, analogy, alliteration, metaphor, allegory, personification, parallels, allusions. They substitute the container for the contained, the sign for the signified, the cause for the effect and vice versa. They employ one name for another; they substitute a part for the whole and the whole for the part; they address the absent as if it were present; they treat the dead as if it were living and call the inanimate as if it were possessed of life; they adapt the sound of the word to its meaning; they affirm a statement by denying its opposite; sometimes they imply a comparison without formally expressing it; sometimes the comparison is a bare suggestion; sometimes it is more sustained.

All this is not just poetic license or linguistic trick, good for ornamentation but bad for correct thinking, as some would warn us. No. These are the ways of saying things effectively. In fact, certain things could not be said otherwise at all.

True, these qualities of a language can be misused. They provide great scope for confusion and misunderstanding. A good deal of literary writing is plain cleverness. It is even deceptive and insincere. Sometimes, one wishes that the language were plainer and more straight. The social sciences, or what goes by that name, are even worse than literature in this respect. Learned jargons hide great ignorance. Pretentious terms, apparently well-defined, are piled one upon another, but they tell precious little. They even confuse and mislead.

All these dangers one would readily concede. But language is an important part of man's higher life and there are greater dangers in neglecting it. It is also a mighty weapon and risks attend upon anything important and significant. These risks multiply if we are arrogant and use words and language in a slipshod, callous, or indifferent manner. But if we go to a language as we go to a temple, if we go to it humbly and in a loving spirit, then it could quicken our understanding and reveal to us new realms of mind and spirit.

Given this attitude, the poets in using different figures of speech, in using language metaphorically and allegorically will do no violence to its spirit. For words by nature are multi-faced and multi-tongued. They report and generalize; they interpret and yield a moral, and suggest unsuspected depths and heights.

And they fulfil this function because they rest and build on the nature of things, because the ideas and things they stand for make it possible, because they express a truth of reality. Words are living because their referents are living. Words speak because the things they stand for are eloquent. What we call the physical world is not dead, nor dumb. It is living; it speaks. It makes suggestions beyond itself. It is penetrated by the life of the Spirit.

There is another reason why words fulfil this function. Words do not merely provide a system of signs for outside things. They express the hidden life of the mind in all its wide ranging. And mind does not live in a world of things and facts and utility; it lives in a world of meanings and significations. Therefore, proper names are only a small part of the vocabulary of a language—and even these are raised up and made to yield larger meanings as we have already seen. An important function of words is to express the larger life of the mind, to express a man's psychic and spiritual life, his motives, hopes, his concepts of right and wrong, life and death, his questions and answers about his whence and whither, his love and worship, his quest for the beyond, the eternal, the infinite, his vision of a perfected life. Indeed, the words that express those concerns are the major and best part of a man's language. A language is not born, as some would like us to believe, of man's small needs and fears and ambitions. Therefore, a vocabulary made of mere expletives, grunts and gasps, words for cooing and wooing and even words naming pots and pans will not do. Language is born out of the fullness of man's heart and, therefore, it must express that fullness. But if it is dragged down to do the opposite, it is denatured.

In their characteristics of being alive, protean, and multifaced, words image the unity of mind and thought in all their heights and depths. Consciousness is not made up of individual thoughts, ideas and concepts. A thought is a part of man's total life-experience and life-style. Therefore, things have not to be merely indicated, they have to have a meaning, a place in man's thought. They have to be related to different parts of man's experience. It is not enough to say, this is a cow, this is sharp, this is sweet. These reports must have some meaning for the thinker, they must convey some truth of the mind. That is why animal-names convey a moral and a wisdom beyond themselves, as we have seen in some of the examples quoted. It is for the same reason that different things mean different things to different people. The word 'night' means one thing to a thief, another to lovers waiting for their tryst, and yet another to a saint or a devotee.

III

In discussing words we found they reveal a great unity. One unity was that of basic sounds, the kind of unity which an ordinary dictionary reveals by arranging words alphabetically.

We observed another unity when discussing the etymologies of words. There we found that one seed-syllable could give rise to a hundred words. For example, the L. *uōx* (compare Skt. *vāk*, speech), a voice, is at the base of such English words as voice, vocal, vowel, vouch, invoke, evoke, revoke, provoke, advocate, vocation, convocation, equivocal. Some of the words that thus come into being have similarity of meanings which can be easily recognized; other meanings have distant, psychological similarities difficult to guess at first sight.

We also noticed another kind of unity between words, a unity between synonyms. A language has generally more than one word to convey the same or nearly the same essential meaning. These words need not be derived from the same root and may not be united phonetically. But they refer to different aspects and suggestions of the same experience. They are words of the same origin, that is, they have been occasioned by the same object—words like burning, flame, furnace, incandescence, conflagration, fever, calory, heat, warmth, glow and shine.

These concepts yield their own larger psychological meanings, and this provides a new point of contact between different words and concepts of a language. Therefore, some of the above words are united, through their psychological meanings, with such different words as ardour, zeal, vigour, energy, passion, enthusiasm, desire, austerity, and life. Similarly, the word 'cold' does not merely indicate a lack of warmth; through its larger psychological meanings, it is related to such words as depressing, cheerless, unemotional, dead, stale, certain, sure.

IV

An ordinary dictionary tries to arrange words according to their alphabetical order. Is there some other way of grouping them, for example, according to their meanings? This kind of grouping could reveal a deep unity within a language, a unity not possible by a system which arranges words only alphabetically.

Roget's *Thesaurus* tries to do it for the English language but the principle should be true for all languages. Here you see, more than anywhere else, that words and ideas are not self-sufficient entities, monads or absolutes which never meet except in confusion—the pet theory of logical positivists. Here you see that words are free wanderers; but their freedom is lawful and their wandering is guided by an inner wisdom. Here you see that words meet and exchange life; they wander and make all kinds of contacts. They are symbols of symbols and stand for each other.

This kind of grouping of words also reveals a great inner coherence in a language, itself based on a deep unity of thought-structure. In fact, words cannot be grouped according to their meanings at all without assuming this unity of thought.

Like sounds, the thought-structure could also be reduced to simpler and more fundamental elements. Perhaps, it could be classified in several ways but the *Thesaurus* does it in the following manner: It divides all thoughts into six categories,[1] these categories into 24 classes, the 24 classes into 1,000 sub-classes.

Then most of the words (theoretically, all) in a language are distributed under these categories and classes according to their meanings. A word does not appear only once, nor only in one category. Since a word has several meanings and these meanings belong to multiple levels, a word appears several times under various categories in association with words of different origin but having similar meanings. These associated words are themselves similarly distributed and have their own associate-words according to their meanings at various levels. In this way, direct and indirect, a word or idea meets other words and ideas at a thousand places.

For example, take the word 'elevation'. It has several meanings and, therefore, it appears several times. In the *Thesaurus* it appears 9 times. In its first meaning it belongs to the Category of

---

[1]These categories are:

i. Category of Abstract Relations (further divided into 8 classes and 178 sub-classes);
ii. Space Category (4 classes and 135 sub-classes);
iii. Category of Matter (3 classes and 113 sub-classes);
iv. Category of Intellect (2 classes and 148 sub-classes);
v. Category of Volition (2 classes and 219 sub-classes);
vi. Category of Sentient and Moral Power (5 classes and 180 sub-classes).

Space. Here also it suggests two ideas, the idea of linear dimension and the idea of motion. Therefore it appears under two different classes of the same category. In both places, it is grouped with dozens of other words of similar meaning like height, altitude, ceiling, eminence, pitch, loftiness or with raising, erection, lifting, upheaval, etc. It also stands for a moral quality as in a phrase like 'elevated mind'. Therefore, the word also appears under the Category of Sentient and Moral Power, in association with a dozen moral qualities which go along with an elevated mind—qualities like generosity, altruism, benevolence, magnanimity, heroism, sublimity, loftiness of purpose, chivalry, devotion, etc.

The word also belongs to the Category of Intellect and in a phrase like 'elevated style', it falls under one of its sub-categories: Communication of Ideas. Here also the word is associated with words that elaborate the sense of an 'elevated style'—bold, glowing, spiritual, pointed, impassioned, lofty, sublime, weighty, eloquent, and so on.

These associate-words are themselves repeated and variously linked with their own associate-words. Therefore, the word 'elevation' will be akin to a thousand words having some meaning and sense in common. These words do not belong to the same family, etymologically speaking; but on that account they are not less related. They reveal an underlying unity of thought which itself is an expression of a deeper psychic and spiritual unity.

CHAPTER 6

Antaḥkaraṇa: Internal Organs of the Mind

In the foregoing chapters, we looked at words in their diversity but they inevitably pointed towards unity. We chose names of ordinary objects like fire, water, cat, dog, trade, tree but, without any prompting on our part or any tortured explanation, they tended to yield larger meanings; they tended to become symbols of a larger reality. We looked at words from the side of objects and the world, but they tended to become thoughts and concepts and invited a look from a more internal station. We restricted ourselves to an empirical approach but the enquiry tended to become philosophical.

We kept to the descriptive approach but the mind sought explanation, the law and reason of things. We imposed on ourselves a limit and stopped short whenever the inquiry tended to go beyond the data of the mind and its legitimate extension beyond the ordinary operation of reason; but we found that the inquiry tended to become a study of thought, of mind, and even of being. So larger meditations cannot be kept out altogether from an inquiry like this. It calls for a philosophical approach. It seeks unity, which is secure and assured, which is rooted in our being.

There are two ways of approaching a language: (*i*) from the side of the world and its objects and (*ii*) from the side of the mind. The first gives an external view; we look at the world from the outside as it were. The second offers a more intimate and inside view. The Western approach, stimulated by its contact with the Sanskrit language in the last century, kept to the first approach; but in India, the second approach too had received its full due in its creative days.

In fact, in Indian thought, man himself is conceived as mind, though mind itself is regarded in a very broad sense. It is thought to be made up of many principles and conceived as functioning on many levels. At one end, it is no more than physical and sensational, *rūpa* and *vedanā*; at the other, it becomes free intelligence, *vijñāna*.

In the long history of Indian Thought and Yoga, these principles have been indicated by different names. In the Upanishads, they have been called *deha*, *prāṇa*, *manas*, *buddhi*; Buddhism has described them as *rūpa*, *vedanā*, *sañjñā*, *saṃskāra*, *vijñāna*. These ideas can roughly be expressed as physical, sensuous, mental and intellectual.

These can further be reduced to three—*indriya* (senses), *manas* (the organ of perception) and *buddhi* (intellect). These taken together are known as *antaḥkaraṇa*, the internal organs of cognition. Putting senses with *manas*, we can reduce their number even to two—*manas* and *buddhi*. Their functions will explain their meanings.

These constituents of the mind make different kinds of contact with the world and know it differently. The seeing of *manas* is not the same as the seeing of *buddhi*. The two have their own characteristic ways of approaching reality. They look for different things. *Manas* looks at an object in its materiality and particularity; *buddhi* as a thought, a concept, an idea. At the level of *indriya* and *manas*, one has the sense of confrontation (*pratigha*) and contact (*sparśa*); but at the level of *buddhi*, this feeling goes and one deals with a reality which is akin to the mind itself. Here too, the objectivity remains but it is of a different kind.

Buddhi has also another meaning in which it reflects, in its purified state, the truths of the Spirit. It is in this sense that the word is used in the Upanishadic and Yogic literature though, in ordinary parlance, it is now used for the conceptualizing and reasoning faculty. In order to avoid this confusion, and in order to render the higher meaning of the word, we shall call it the spiritual faculty. It is an important faculty and words derive their deeper meaning from this faculty.

A language reflects this peculiarity and structure of the mind.

The different principles of mind contribute different words to a language and also different layers of meanings to the same word.

If we look at words, we find that they belong to different categories, answering to different organs of the mind. Some are predominantly *manas*-words; some are *buddhi*-words. Some are names of physical objects like a table or a chair. Even at this level, there are various degrees of abstraction. Some are merely proper names; some are names of a class of common objects; some indicate a group of objects taken collectively—words like 'troop' and 'administration'; some words like 'water' or 'air' or 'iron' do not refer to discrete objects, but they indicate material objects whose nature is rather pervasive and elemental.

As one penetrates deeper, one leaves behind individual objects of ordinary experience and enters into the world of functions and structure, as in modern physical sciences. Here the names become symbols. Though these symbols refer to a non-sensuous reality, the reality still remains physical though at a very subtle level.

Other non-sensible words like 'forces of production' take a different direction and belong to a conceptual and intellectual order. Some non-sensuous words like 'class' or 'nation' do not refer to people who share common physical qualities but to people who share a common consciousness of identity.

Along with this generalizing and conceptualizing process of the mind, there is also an internalizing process. Some experiences have utility for us; or they are associated with pleasant or painful memories. In this way, they become psychologically significant for us; they become internalized. Even the meanest and most ordinary objects are capable of this alchemy. They become associated with our emotional and affectional mind and thus they enter our *prāṇa-kośa* (vital mind) and get assimilated by it. The words that stand for them also refer to the experiences and emotions they occasion in us.

There are other words which are names, not of physical objects, not even of utilitarian goods or even of emotionally charged experiences, but they stand for some deep psychic qualities in the individual. Words like mother, father, friend, neighbour, country, citizen belong to this category. The sensuous mind could give us words like man and woman but not father and mother or husband and wife or brother and sister—these derive from a psychic source and incarnate a deep soul-quality. In these higher mean-ings, motherhood, for example, is not mere viviparity and father-hood is not just a capacity for planting children.

There are other words which refer to objects only apparently physical—words like plants, trees, rivers. We are ourselves plants and water and, therefore, we secretly respond to them in an intimate way. Similarly, the elements like the earth, fire, the sky, the sun are already within us and, therefore, our response to these words is intimate.

In fact, all deeper truths of life are psychic. They already reside in the psyche. The experience of the outside world merely helps to illumine the psyche, reminds it of its own truths.

In the same way, every truth, even the most physical, is capable of being converted into a psychic truth. And the psyche too illumines the physical. Without the psyche, the experience of the physical world is nothing. Only in its lowest meaning does experience mean merely capacity for sensation and feeling, *vedanā*. But the physical world is still important; for as things are on the terrestrial plane, the path of self-discovery and God-discovery lies through world-discovery.

Some of the most significant words in a language like non-violence, justice, truth, forgiveness refer to the moral nature of man. These too are psychic truths. They have a universality and they make a direct appeal to the purified *buddhi*. They rise above the immediate, narrow motives. They are not ego-centred. They are centred in others, or, more truly, in our higher nature. They are *disinterested*.

Again, words like love, compassion, service too have a similar spiritual source. In their less pure states, they still have a vital content and, therefore, easy to understand by the vital mind. But as the mind gets more purified, their meanings become deeper and more psychic. Their true meanings appear when the violence, passions and appetites of the mind have subsided.

Some words like *dama* (self-restraint), *śama* (tranquility), and *śānti* (peace) are Yogic words. They are not even entertained by the vital mind. They are looked with askance by it. Similarly, words like *dhyāna* (reflection), *dhāraṇā* (continued meditation), *samādhi* (absorption) make no apparent sense. In the ordinary course, they form no part of man's experience, moral or intellectual. And yet they are the very staple of a higher life.

For the same reason, truths like *asteya* (non-stealing) and *aparigraha* (non-possession) are indicated negatively. For, ordinarily, people know non-stealing and non-possession indirectly, through stealing and possession. Direct experience of them comes only when the current of life is reversed, when the Gaṅgā begins to flow upward towards its source.

III

But this presentation is not strictly exact. There are no exclusive words in a language representing only one principle. These principles co-exist and work together. A word carries within it simultaneously all the different meanings of the different ways in which different organs of the mind make their contact with the world. A word refers to an object which the *manas* contacts through the senses; it also refers to the feeling which the object occasions; it indicates its class; it indicates the idea for which the object stands; and it also stands for the psychic truth which the object embodies.

Thus the mind, through its different organs, particularizes, generalizes, conceptualizes, symbolizes. It sees an object as an individual, as a member of a class, as a symbol of something larger. It sees in objects qualities which they share with one another. At a still more subtle level, it sees them as embodiments of its own attributes, as its own projections and self-formations. A word has to carry all these meanings. It has to stand for an object, a feeling, an idea, a truth of the Spirit.

So there is no word which is purely a physical referent, lacking larger, intellectual and psychic meanings. What can be said with justice is that there are certain words, like table or chair, in which sensuous contact plays a larger role, while words like friendship and justice indicate magnitudes which are more intellectual. With the same justness, one could maintain that there are many people whose minds are more physical and sensuous and in whom the intellectual principle is not strong. To such minds, a language is no more than a glossary, a catalogue of names of physical objects and activities.

But leaving aside exceptional cases, for most of the people and for most of the time, words have multiple meanings and even the commonest words at their most sensuous have larger meanings. And these meanings are not arbitrary; they follow from the very structure of the mind, the way it is constituted and the way it works. It is because of this peculiarity of the mind that words acquire capacity for multi-faced existence, are capable of extension in many directions, rise from the particular to the general, from the name of an object to the name of a quality, from the concrete to the abstract, from the objective to the subjective, from the sensuous to the mental, from the existential to the essential and intellectual. Lower meanings are taken up into the higher and used for a new purpose.

Let us take, for illustration, a word like 'thorn'. In its most rudimentary meaning, the word is a referent and points to a physical object. But in this limited sense, the word will have hardly any utility. It has to have a wider meaning and must, at least, be able to denote a class if it is to be worth anything.

The question of the relationship of the particular with the general has engaged the attention of a whole array of philosophers, but it need not detain us here. It suffices to say that if the mind has more than one power, and if it is constituted of more than one principle, then it can perform both these and many other functions simultaneously. While the general includes the particular, the particular also stands for the general. The mind often thinks in terms of images, though thought is more than images. If thought were imprisoned in images, it would fail in its function. A thought is more than a particular image; it must go beyond it to convey larger meanings.

Now, continuing our illustration, a thorn first refers to an object like a brier or a prickle which is sharp and pointed. Then at second remove, it can refer to anything that shares those qualities, like nails and needles. Thus the name of a thing becomes the name of a quality and then by a transferred use a name of all objects that share that quality.

The name also rises from an objective cognition to a feeling. It could refer to the painful experience that sharp, pointed things occasion when they impinge on the sense of touch. A thorn pricks but pricking shares a certain similarity of sensation with the experiences of stinging, piercing, biting, cutting. All these experiences have their own overtones, but they share a common quality of being 'sharp'. 'Sharp' itself is probably allied to 'scrape' which means shaving, scratching, or removing a surface with a sharp instrument. 'Stinging' is from Gk. *stachys*, spike of grain; some say it is allied to 'stick' and 'stake'. 'Piercing' is from L. *pertundere*, to thrust through or bore through. 'Biting' is seizing and cleaving, chiefly with teeth. It derives from Skt. *bhid*, to break, divide. 'Cutting' derives from the experience of an edged instrument piercing something. This gives us the Swedish *kuta*, a knife; or Icelandic *kuti*, a little knife; or Norwegian *kyttel* or *kiutul*, which means a knife for barking trees.

Thus the word 'thorn' enlarges its meaning. From being a name of a particular physical object, it begins to stand for a certain characteristic sensation which that object occasions; then, through a certain quality which this sensation shares with other similar sensations, it acquires a new membership in a larger club where it rubs shoulders with other members like stick, stake, knife, etc.

The process of enlargement does not stop here. The sharp, piercing pain caused by a thorn could stand for any pain, any feeling of distress, vexation and irritation. Eventually, it could stand for anything which has a sting in it, which is ticklish, difficult, or intricate or challenging. Thus we speak of thorny ground, thorny situations, thorny arguments, thorny problems, and even a crown of thorns. In all these uses, the word rises in meaning from the physical to the sensuous, to the mental, to the intellectual.

IV

The Sāṃkhya philosophy presents these ideas more systematically. Its epistemology derives from its ontology. We need not discuss it here at any length but only mention those features which are relevant to the present thesis.

Sāṃkhya moves from the subtle to the gross. It posits an undifferentiated Primordial Reality *(avyakta, prakṛti)* which in its first modification is more like mind than matter. This very first formation is called *buddhi* or *mahat*, Intelligence, Vast. In its turn, this gives birth to the principle of *ahaṃkāra*, Individuation or Ego. Ego bifurcates. It becomes both the spectator as well as the spectacle, the mind *(manas)*, and the senses (*indriya*), as well as the vision, the object. So, in a way, the perceiver and the perceived are the same. They have a common matrix. If the two were exclusive, the mind could not know its objects. So, in a way, a man's world is also a selection. The senses see what is akin to them; and the object (*rūpa*) they know already partakes of the reality of the senses and the *manas*.

All objects of an *indriya* or sense meet in that *indriya*. As the *Bṛhadāraṇyaka Upaniṣad*[1] says, the uniting point of all forms is the eye, of all smells the nostril, of all sounds the ear. But as we move further, all sense-experiences meet in the *manas*. In fact, it is not the eyes that see but the *manas;* it is not ears that hear but the *manas*. Different senses bring their reports to the *manas* and the *manas* imposes its unity on them. However different these sense reports may be, they meet in the *manas* and receive its imprint. They may still retain the flavour of their origin but in the *manas* they become interchangeable.

All objects meet in the senses and all sense-experiences meet in the *manas*. The first is easy enough to understand. But what to make of the second statement?

Let us make the point clearer by a few examples. First, take the word 'sharp'. It is akin to Old English *scieran*, to cut. It is a word

---

[1]2.4.11.

essentially depicting a tactile experience but it can also be used to characterize an experience proper to the ear as in the phrase 'sharp notes'; or to experiences of the eye or tongue or nose as in phrases like 'sharp looks', 'sharp flavour' or 'sharp odour'. It can also be used to denote a quality of the mind itself as in 'sharp temper' and 'sharp mind'.

Similarly, the words 'loud' and 'clear' are, on the level of senses, experiences of the ear. 'Loud' is akin to Gk. *klutes*, renowned, and Skt. *śrutas*, famous, heard, from, *śru*, to hear; but it is also used in phrases like 'loud appearance' and 'loud smell', experiences of the eye and the nose. The word 'clear' derives from L. *clārus*, clear in sound (akin to the *clamāre*, to cry out), but it can also characterize experiences of different origins. It now means bright, luminous, transparent, pure, serene, plain. We speak of a man's clear views, clear mind, clear character; we also speak of clear weather, a clear road and a clear profit.

'Sour' means rank and rancid which applies fundamentally to taste. But we also speak of sour notes (jarring), and sour looks (cross or sullen). Similarly, 'sweet' is akin to L. *suavi*, Gk. *hēdus*, Skt. *svad*, to taste, to eat. It fundamentally denotes a tongue experience but we now speak of sweet looks, sweet notes, sweet smells, sweet words, etc.

Some words convey, even in their roots, two senses and experiences; one of the mind itself and the other of sense which changes into the former in any case. For example, the Latin word *sapare* means both to taste as well as to discern, or to know. So, this has given us words like 'saporous', 'sapience', and 'savant' which belong to different orders. 'Saporous' belongs essentially to the sense of tongue; 'savant' and 'sapience' refer to qualities of the mind.

The word 'sagacious' is akin to L. *sāgīre,* which means to perceive clearly, to perceive by senses, perhaps to scent. But now the word means a man of far-sighted and penetrating judgement, which denotes a quality of the mind.

The Skt. *vid*, to know, has two senses, as we see in its two Greek variants—*eidenai*, to know, and *idein,* to see. Its Old High

German equivalent *wizze*, knowledge, carries the first sense; the L. *uidere*, to see, carries the second meaning. So, while in Sanskrit, the root gives us the words *vidyā,* knowledge, and *veda*, the Vedas, in English, from the two senses of the same root, we have words like vision, view, vista, visit, in which the sense of seeing predominates; and also words like wisdom, idea, wit, in which the sense of knowing predominates.

The *manas* is not only the meeting-point of all organs of sense-knowledge but also the meeting and starting point of all organs of actions. We do not say, 'my hands work', or 'my legs walk', but both are referred back to an entity 'I', which both works and walks.

The *manas* also unites the receptive and the expressive functions of the mind and reconciles knowing with doing. The Sanskrit root *jnā*, to know, has an Anglo-Saxon form *cunnan*, which means both 'to know' as well as 'be able', or 'to know how to do'. Its Swedish form *kunna* means 'to know', and also 'to be able'. So this root has given us not only the word 'knowledge' but also the words 'can' and 'cunning', which in its older sense meant skill. It is in this sense that the word is used in the Bible: "If I forget thee, O Jerusalem, let my right hand forget her cunning."[2]

For further illustration, we can take the word 'do' itself. It is supposed to derive from a Sanskrit root *dhā*, to place, put; or its Greek form *tithenai*, to place, set. These roots have given us not only the word 'do' and 'deeds' but also 'deem' and 'doom'. While 'do' means to act, 'deem' means to think, judge, suppose. 'Deed' is action; 'doom' is judgement as in Old English *dōmes daeg*, day of judgement.

So every piece of knowledge is also action and vice versa; and behind both deed and dream, action and thought is the same power of consciousness.

V

Now we move from the *manas* to the *buddhi*. As senses bring their data to the *manas*, *manas* brings its data to the *buddhi*. As

[2]The Old Testament, Psalms, 137.5.

manas gives unity to the sense-data, *buddhi* does the same to the *manas*-data though on a still higher plane. It raises that data from the level of perception to the level of conception and understanding. It rejects in it all that is sensuous and particular and converts it into the ideal, the abstract, and the essential.

The *buddhi*-knowledge is no longer tied to sensuous images and particular instances though it may still use them. But it works best when it is no longer burdened by them; when, in fact, the eyes are closed. In this new form, it acquires a new mobility, efficiency, versatility and unity. Its different elements can be sifted and separated and combined in many new ways. They can be stored, communicated and transmitted. They become evocative. If and when necessary, they could summon the essential images. We cannot carry physical objects with us, but we can carry their images. But even images become blurred with time; fortunately, we can store them too and carry them as 'ideas', or carry what they signify.

In short, *buddhi*-knowledge is freer; but this freedom does not make it capricious. In fact, it brings it under the discipline of necessity, the necessity of law and rationality. *Manas*-knowledge simply *is*; but *buddhi*-knowledge *has to be*. In philosophical language, *manas*-knowledge is 'contingent' but *buddhi*-knowledge is 'necessary'.

So *buddhi*-knowledge is not merely an extension of *manas*-knowledge; it has a new dimension, a new character and characteristic, a new use, capability and power. It gives us conceptual and rational knowledge. In this sense, it is known as Reason in the West. But in Sāṃkhya, *buddhi* has a still higher existence. In this mode it is a principle of *direct seeing*, not so much of logical inference. But let us not discuss it here.

The *buddhi*-level of meanings too is reflected in a word. Going back to our illustration of 'thorn', it is both a *manas*-word as well as a *buddhi*-word. At the *manas* level, it refers to a particular object. At the level of lower *buddhi*, it becomes a name of a whole class of similar objects; but at a still higher rung of *buddhi*, it becomes a name of an 'idea'.

As an 'idea', it may still use the image of a thorn but in fact it is referring to an entirely different thing. For example, in phrases like 'to stand or walk upon thorns' (be in a painful state of anxiety or suspense), or 'to sit upon thorns' (to fret and chafe), the physical referent has already a secondary place. Here the idea is more fundamental. It is also independent of the image it uses. In fact, it could express itself by widely different images, even by those which exclude the thorn-image.

For example, the general idea of 'a thorn in the side' could be expressed by very different images like 'a snake in the grass', or 'a skeleton in the cupboard'. Thus thorn as an idea is very different from thorn as an object. As an idea, it acquires a new independence and enters a larger world; it is also used in a richer context; and it is also more 'ideal' in content.

Buddhi has this independence because it *sees* more. While *manas* only sees what is presented to it, *buddhi* can stand aloof behind *manas*-experiences and see what they signify and how they stand in relation to each other. For example, every feeling is accompanied by many bodily correlates; *buddhi* sees this fact and utilizes it for its own freedom. To illustrate, a strong feeling of fear could make a man's blood run cold, or chill his spine, or make his flesh creep, or make his hair stand on end, or make his body tremble, or make his heart sink, or make him sweat, or make him turn pale or white. *Buddhi* sees all this and, therefore, it could make use of any of these images in order to say something about the same feeling. It is not limited by one image alone.

Similarly, on the expressive side, a man could show his dislike or dissent by shaking his head, or shrugging his shoulders, or by looking askance; and he could express his resentment by knitting his brows, or by stamping his feet, or by clenching his teeth or fist, or by exploding, or by looking daggers. *Buddhi* sees all this and more, and, therefore, could use, with its own judgement of appropriateness, any of these images to express the idea of disapproval or dissent or resentment or revolt.

The truth of this point does not change if instead of the same feeling expressing itself in different physiological correlates, we have the same physiognomy expressing different feelings and different states of mind. The face, for example, is an index of the mind. It could brighten up at one feeling; and it could turn red or black or pale at another. Similarly, one feeling or thought could make a man's blood rise; another could turn it cold. But it is for *buddhi* to decide how to make use of these images, or whether or not to make use of them at all, or whether to express its thoughts in an entirely different language. *Buddhi* retains its freedom.

VI

Thus Sāṃkhya gives us a unified and ordered theory of all knowledge and meanings. All objects of the senses meet in their respective senses and all sense-experiences meet in the *manas.* However different they may be from their own angles, they are the same for the *manas,* and it uses them interchangeably. The *manas*-data, in turn, is *buddhi's* raw material and *buddhi* uses it in its own free way and in accordance with its own nature. It rejects, chooses, reshapes, rearranges, reintegrates, reinterprets. Sāṃkhya shows how the physical and physiological meanings are held in the affectional, and the affectional and the sensuous in the conceptual; the last in turn is held in the intellectual. A word carries meanings belonging to these different orders.

Sāṃkhya also provides simultaneously for two opposite movements. It shows how consciousness moves from the physical to the psychological and the intellectual and also from the intellectual to the psychological and the physical.

In life, in ordinary human development, the physical or the sensuous mind comes first; and in most cases, it also remains predominant. To this mind, a word is primarily a name of a physical object or a strong emotion; and any other, more psychological and intellectual meaning is merely an extension of the primary meaning. But in the statement of principles, *tattvas*, and to a mind that has turned inward, and has developed a capacity for seeing from *within*, the order is reversed. The physical and the sensuous worlds reflect inner realities; outer objects convey information about inner states of mind. They represent, in a physical and sensuous form, the 'idea', some universal truth of the deeper psyche and mind. To this mind, the sky is an image of the Infinity within, which could also be evoked by the image of the ocean, or of stars, or even by mathematical numbers. So, for this mind, the sky, the ocean, the stars are as much metaphors as are the ideas of infinity and eternity to another kind of mind if by metaphor we mean a transferred meaning, a transliteration of meaning from one language to another, from the language of one level of mind to that of another.

So, to an inward mind, words change radically in their meanings and significance. To this mind, they convey a different order of meanings and reveal certain truths which already live in the psyche. When the soul awakens, all seeing becomes soul-seeing. But this seeing does not negate other seeings and other meanings; on the contrary, it unites them and raises them up and provides a new comprehension and a new perspective. It shows how different layers of meanings of a word interpenetrate; with what ease they move from the physical to the intellectual, up and down, back and forth; how the particular and the universal meet; how the most concrete can express the most abstract and how the most abstract can be invoked by the most concrete; and how they all express the truth of the Spirit.

CHAPTER 7

Bhūmis: Levels of Purity

Words derive their meanings from different organs of the mind. They are modified by the fact that these organs work together and their meanings interpenetrate. But there is also another dimension of the problem. Different organs function at different levels of purity and this factor radically changes the meanings of words.

According to Sāṃkhya, the mind, its different organs and states, have three qualities: *tamas*, *rajas* and *sattva*. The first quality makes the mind dull and obscure; the second makes it restless and passionate; but the third quality endows it with purity and clarity. These affect the working of the mind. And though the mind may use the same words, every level of purity puts its own meaning into them.

According to the Yogas, both of Patañjali as well as of the Buddhists, the mind functions at two levels (*bhūmis*) of purity. These are called *kāma-bhūmi* (the sensuous plane) and *dhyāna bhūmi* (the contemplative plane). These have their own sub-divisions, each having its own degree of purity and inwardness, but these two are the main divisions.

In the first, *kāma-bhūmi*, the desire-principle predominates. It is characterized by passionate attachments and aversions; it is opaque and dull, and also dissipated and restless. These qualities keep the mind bound to the lower meanings of the word. But as desire drops, one acquires increasingly more purity, and enters into *dhyāna-bhūmi*, the meditative level. Here the mind is *ekāgra*, ingathered and concentrated. This brings to us the luminous forms of things and reveals their higher meanings.

In Indian philosophical thought, all phenomenal reality is called *nāma-rūpa,* or Subject and Object, Thought and Things. Now *nāma* and *rūpa* go together. They share the quality and purity of the level to which they belong. On the level of *kāma*, where desire dominates, both are impure. *Rūpa* is obscure and so are its mental correlates. But when the mind is purified, when its more clamorous attractions and aversions subside, when it becomes more settled and calm, its vision too becomes clearer. Desire-forms leave and yield place to more subtle and more joyous underlying forms, even to still more basic thought-forms.

As a result, words too carry the meanings of the level of consciousness from which they derive. Those belonging to *kāma-bhūmi*, have merely surface meanings; these meanings are loud and external; they tell nothing deep about what they denote. The sound-signs attached to them are conventional.

II

In earlier chapters we have already seen that even a most lowly word is capable of having a higher meaning. But, unfortunately, its reverse also is true. However exalted a word may appear to be, from whatever organ of the mind it may originate, it too is capable of a lower meaning put into it by a desire-mind. No word, even though it may belong to the highest ethical and religious vocabulary, is free from the operation of this law. A desire-dominated mind suffers in its power of perception and interpretation and this gives limited and outer meanings to words.

Some people think that there are secular words with their lower meanings and spiritual words with their higher meanings. But, if what we have been discussing is properly understood, then it is not so. There are no secular and spiritual words as such but only a secular and spiritual understanding of them.

This explains the fact that while certain words and ideas are common to widely different religious cultures, they are not understood in the same way by them. And even within the same culture, they do not have the same meanings. They mean different things to different people. And even the fact that they belong to the religious vocabulary does not prevent them from being understood and used in most unedifying ways.

The deterioration in meanings that words of religious and spiritual import like Self, Brahma, God, Soul, and Truth suffer is of many kinds and degrees. The one most common is *tāmasika*. The words become too familiar; they get stereotyped; they become innocuous; they no longer quicken, agitate, challenge. The spirit leaves them. Their meanings contract to the ordinary life of getting and spending. They no longer have a transforming influence.

This deterioration has also a social facet to which Marx made a pointed reference. Religious ideas and institutions become opiates of the people. They lull them to sleep.

There is a *rājasika* deterioration too. The truths of the Spirit are used for self-aggrandisement, for self-promotion. Socially they become ideologies of ruling classes and nations, rationalizations of their interests. Here God becomes a desire-God, an Ego-God, a God of a particular tribe or church trying to become the God of mankind through propaganda, through high salesmanship, through crusades, proselytizing, wars. Here the devotees worship and love their God with all their sword-strength, with all their mind-cunning of theology, with all their soul-sob and heart-heat.

In religious cultures which make exclusive claims for their god, scripture or prophet, these words carry within them ego-satisfying meanings. On this point, Roget's *Thesaurus* yields some very interesting data. It provides a kind of ideograph of the Christian mind, at least of the English-speaking Christian world. In this mind, the word 'revelation', for example, arouses connected pictures of the "Word, Word of God, Scripture, Bible, Book of Books, Inspired Writings, etc."; but the word 'Pseudo-Revelation', on the other hand, inspires the following ideas: "Koran, Alcoran, Ly-king, Shaster, Vedas, Zend-Avesta, Vendidad, Purana, Gautam Buddha, Book of Mormon, etc.".

Similarly, the word 'Deity' subsumes the ideas of "God, Lord, Jehovah, Holy Trinity, God the Son, the Messiah, the Wise, the

Merciful"; but the words like "Allah, Brahma, Vishnu, Shiva, Krishna" are grouped together with "Baal, Thor, Mumbo-Jumbo, Nixie-Pixy, Kalie, etc." No wonder that to this mind, 'false prophet' means "Buddha, Zoroaster, Confucius, Mahomet".[1]

So it is not that the people at the *kāma-bhumi* have no Gods, no worship, no value-system, no compassion, no truth but their meanings are pretty mixed up. We can observe this fact in our daily life. We see people and parties invoking the high values of liberty, equality, and fraternity but in their names they practise colonialism, wars of liberation, mass liquidation, unequal treaties, slave labour camps, thought control.

The same is true in the religious sphere. In fact, many religions have been pronouncedly political and ideological and many ideologies have generated religious fervour. If we study religious words from this viewpoint, they provide interesting psychological, sociological and historical data. They tell us how they rationalize and justify self-interest; how they support egoism; they tell us of class and national interests masquerading in religious garb. The different names and conceptions of Gods tell us the story of the rise and fall of different empires and cultures—how different Gods were dethroned when their champions were dethroned; how this changed the meaning and emotions connected with their cults and worship. Take, for example, the word 'orgy'. Once it had a deep meaning. The word is derived from the Gk. *orgion*, a sacred act or rite. It was the name of acts of secret

---

[1]The picture the *Theasaurus* presents is somewhat old and, probably, it would not be so intolerant if it were drawn to-day. And even in the past, Christianity did not invoke uniformity a self-congratulatory picture even amongst its own votaries. There were sectarian wars and to many Protestant reformers, the Church meant 'Popery, Scarlet Lady, the Whore of Rome'. To the Catholics, Protestantism was 'schism, apostasy, atheism, bibliolatry'. And to the rationalists of the Age of Reason, Christianity itself of whatever hue was 'bigotry, credulity, fanaticism, superstition, sanctimonious hypocrisy'.

And if the Red indians, the Africans and the Asians were also in the habit of writing their own Thesauruses, they would add to the above the ideas of 'genocide, imperialism, Maxim guns, white man's burden, bribes, proselytizing, warring sect, etc'.

worship practised by the initiates, just like mystery rites. These rites related to the worship of Demeter, Orpheus but most commonly of Bacchus. But when these Gods fell before the new, rising Christian God, the word acquired a new meaning—revelry and drunkenness.

III

Most of the time, a language expresses a man's gall and spleen. People use contentious words, flattering words, lying words. They swear, backbite, scorn. They use words for feeding their own ego, for flattering the powerful and for hurting the weak. With every word they speak, they brag whether they know it or not. They blow hot and cold in the same breath. Their first word is contradicted by their next. Every word they use is a mask, a lie and is meant to conceal rather than to reveal. They talk ill, find fault, wrangle about nothing.

In still many more cases, when their words are not violent or offensive, they are still inane. People merely gossip and prate. Though they talk so much, yet they have so little to say. This is true particularly of academicians and faculty men. They speak mechanically, compulsively, in jargons. They use big words for small things. Their debates, seminars and workshops are nothing but words reacting to words with little sense of relevance and reality.

The words people use express, for most of the time, man's essential thoughtlessness, the ordinariness of his soul and the triviality of his interests. They express his malice, his pride and his unrest. As a result, they lose much of their usefulness for expressing man's higher life. For this reason, they have invited the suspicion and distrust of the sages. Competent teachers have repeatedly warned against mere words, words that hurt, that tell nothing, the letter that killeth as opposed to the spirit that quickens.

But the warning is not against the words as such; it is against their lower meanings and outward use. Healing words, revealing words are welcome. The spiritual teachers celebrate 'the mouth of a righteous man',[2] which they liken to a 'well of life'. They hold that 'the wholesome tongue is a tree of life'.[3]

But alas! all mouths are not righteous and all tongues are not wholesome. Words have a lower meaning and a lower use too. Most of the time, most of the people do not refrain from making a lower use of words in their lower meanings.

IV

Above we have spoken mostly of the *tāmasika* and *rājasika* degeneration of meanings. This kind of degeneration is easy to spot. To the *Chāndogya Upaniṣad*, 'quarrellers, tale-bearers and slanderers' are 'small men', *alpāḥ kalahinaḥ piṣunā apavādinaḥ.*[4] Similarly, those who bear false witness and sow 'discord among brethren'[5] are abominations to the God of the Jews. Those who are 'faithless in their mouth', and who 'flatter with their tongue, ... their throat is an open sepulchre'.[6] And though their words are 'smoother than butter', or 'softer than oil', but in reality they are like a 'drawn sword'.[7]

When the language is openly abusive, spiteful, virulent or malicious or false, impurity is easy to locate. But impurity exists at a more *sāttvika* level too, for *sattva* has still a goodly mixture of the *rajas* and the *tamas*. It exists even in the thoughts and works of the poets, legislators and philosophers of great renown.

As a man rises above ordinary desires, utilities, likes and dislikes, he enters into a state of mind which is more imaginative and intellective. Here words acquire different meanings. They become symbols. They evoke suggestive images and convey unsuspected shades of meanings. They have a mood, an aura, a sphere of influence. They modify the meanings of other words with which they associate or which come into their orbit. All these

---

[2]The Old Testament, Proverbs, 10-11.

[3]Ibid., 15.4.

[4]7.6.1

[5]The Old Testament, Proverbs, 16.7.9

[6]Ibid., Psalms, 5, 9.

[7]Ibid., 55.21.

things cannot be defined concretely but they can easily be intuited by sensitive minds. Poets make effective use of this layer of meanings.

Some of the best literature of a nation belongs to this group which uses words in their subtle suggestions and meanings. Through them a good poet or writer could make a man weep or laugh and live through a whole gamut of emotions and ideas. He could make one live certain emotions in imagination which it would be inconvenient and even impossible to live in life. He could also help men live their emotions at a level of intensity which has a certain deepening effect; this raises them from a vegetative existence and gives them a sense of authenticity which they otherwise lack.

But this has its negative aspect too. This literature, particularly when it is not saved by a higher vision, becomes a substitute for reality. In this literature, there could be a good deal of dreaming and make-believe, wishing and pretending, cloying sentimentality and sweetness against which more sensitive souls revolt. In fact, there is already a good deal of revolt which is giving birth to a new literature. In order to escape the vague, the indolent, the dreamy, the cloyingly sentimental, the never never land of the lotus-eaters, the land of eternal kisses and embracing, many writers have taken to experimenting with a new kind of hard-headed intellectuality. They even explore the morbid and the sordid, the trivial, the inane in order to feel the touch of the real and to evoke the sensation of depth and solidity. That they miss the real is another matter. For what they have embraced is not the real but the shadow of the real.

There is another danger too. The meanings here have a quality of far-away suggestions and echoes, of floating and ethereal forms. But these could be misleading. Their subtle meanings could be mistaken by many for the celestial. But they are not the light above, only the shadow of the light.

A poet may use words for their softer and gentler suggestions and meanings in order to evoke a picture of mildness and delicacy and a twilight world made of dream-stuff. But at another level, words have also more stable and granitoid meanings, meanings which cannot be pulled or pushed and coaxed. These are spiritual meanings revealed to a mind which has attained a certain level of purity, freedom and equanimity and self-status.

V

To this mixed variety also belongs another impurity which comes in when a man's words are larger than his experience. Here, no active evil is involved and probably the speaker means well. But he speaks words wiser than he knows and deeper than he feels. This lends to his speech a quality which though unintended is quite jarring. He speaks without authority.

Socrates was very sensitive to this impurity of speech. He found that the poets, legislators and philosophers spoke not foolishly but over-wisely. They spoke what they did not understand, what was unsupported by their experience and life.

This is a very common impurity. People speak words of wisdom without being wise; they speak brave words without being brave. They speak of intensities they do not feel; they speak words they do not understand. They are unauthentic.

Shri Krishna warns against flowery language, *puṣpitām vācam*[8] and also against those given to quoting from the scriptures thoughtlessly, *vedavādaratāḥ*.[9] The talent for quotation is a poor substitute for the understanding of the heart.

Some interpret this warning too sweepingly and turn it into a denunciation of all scriptures and teachings. But the warning is meant only against those who are given to the outer meanings of scriptural truths, who speak wiser than they know, *prajñā-vādānśca bhāṣase*,[10] those who use big words to express small truths of life. So the *Gitā's* warning is not against the scriptures but against those who approach them without adequate humility and preparation, in the spirit of contention, in the pride of learning. Scriptural words speak with many tongues. There is something

---

[8]*Bhagvadgītā*, 2.42

[9]Ibid.

[10]Ibid., 2.11

which they convey through the spoken word but there is a good deal more which they convey through the voice of silence. An active, cogitating mind is kept out of their inner meanings.

It is said of al-Ghazzali, an illustrious Muslim theologian of his times, that one day he was speaking to an audience on the subject of God. In the middle of his speech, he fell silent and remained speechless for many, many months. Later on, when speech returned to him, he explained that while he was speaking, a voice descended on him and asked, "What do you know of what you are talking about?" The question came to him with such force that he was struck dumb.

The more one goes into the depth of a word and sees its hidden meanings, the quieter one becomes. "A gentleman is ashamed that his words are better than his deeds," says Confucius.[11] Yes, not only better than his deeds but also wiser than his meanings and better than his intentions.

But people of *rajas* and *tamas*, people who do not care about being as good as their words, people suffering from numbness of heart and mind, people who are tone-deaf to higher suggestions are loquacious. On the other hand, people who have modesty, truth and spiritual perception weigh and watch out every word. They are frugal in their speech because they know that speech is a portion of themselves. They know that in the presence of words, they are on holy ground and they must use them with reverence and circumspection. They know that words have also a deep nature and are pregnant with deep meanings which can be understood and communicated through deep soul-churning. One has to learn to open out to those meanings.

VI

Beyond this lies *dhyāna-bhūmi* or *ekāgra-bhūmi*. As the mind acquires purity and one-pointedness, desire-forms begin to melt and in their place is revealed a more luminous world of objects. As one separates oneself from lower desires and motivations,

---

[11]*The Wisdom of Confucius*, The Modern Library, New York, p. 193.

the words also drop their lower associations and meanings. As the mind learns to be more concentrated, its seeing becomes more concentrated, penetrating, more essential. It sees more of an object as it were. The object shines with a new light.

As meditation deepens and equanimity grows, one finds that the light of the object is mind's own light. Words now refer to a reality which is more akin to mind than to matter.

Sāṃkhya tells us that it is not the eyes that see but it is the seeing that creates the eyes, the *cakṣu-āyatana.* The purified mind moves to subtler levels of reality and words also refer to these subtler levels. Their meanings move from the object to the eye and then to the seer; in the language of the Pātañjala Yoga, they move from *grāhya* (object) to *grahaṇa* (*antaḥkaraṇa*), to *gṛihītṛ* (observer). In the process of ascent, the words lose their ordinary verbal form, and even their thought-form.

At a still deeper level of purity and impersonality, they begin to point to the Unmanifest in the manifest, the Non-being in the being, the Imperishable in the perishable, the Unspeakable and the Silent in the spoken, the Nameless in the name.

On this *bhūmi*, the language also acquires meanings proper to its higher nature and function. Here words are not used to hurt or spite or curse but to heal and soothe and bless. Here words bring succour; they wipe away tears of despair and bring hope and joy. Here the tongue also speaks in defence of *dharma* (the right and the true), and against *adharma* (the wrong and the false). Here words express the gratitude of a thankful heart; they sing of man's love of the remote and the infinite and the pure; in short, they express the Gods within. When a man reaches the purity of the Self, he becomes a *sāmaga*, a singer of the *Sāmaveda—sāma gāyannāste*—as the Upanishads put it.[12]

---

[12]*Taittirīya Upaniṣad*, 3.10.4.

CHAPTER 8

Higher Meanings: Their Secret Abode and Secret Key

As words are capable of expressing deep meanings, they are eminently suited for expressing man's higher life. In fact, they are in their most proper form when they perform that function. When put to lower uses, they become denatured and, therefore, false.

A word is as high and deep and also as shallow and outward as man's mind. On the one hand, it hardly touches the surface of human experience; on the other, it sounds its very depth. Its body is made up of the earth but its soul is of the stuff of heaven.

If words have these high meanings and this holiness, some important questions arise in the mind: Where do these meanings reside? Why are they not so self-evident? How can they be unlocked?

The answer to the first question given by the mystic tradition is cryptic. The *Ṛgveda* speaks of the secret Name, *nāma apīcyam*,[1] it speaks of secret words, *niṇyā vācāñsi*,[2] and secret Names, *nāmāni guhyā*.[3] It says that the Speech, surrounded by a thousand syllables, *sahasrākṣarā*,[4] resides in the highest region of heaven, *parame vyomani*.

According to this tradition, a word has deep roots in our being and its greater life is hidden there. Like an iceberg, it shows only a part of itself. The *Ṛgveda* says that a word exists at four levels and three of them are hidden in the cave of the heart, *guhā trīṇi nihitā*.[5]

---

[1]*Ṛgveda*, 2.35.11 [2]Ibid., 4.3.16

[3]Ibid., 8.41.5 [4]Ibid., 1.164.41

[5]चत्वारि वाक् परिमिता पदानि तानि विदुर्ब्राह्मणा ये मनीषिणः ।
गुहा त्रीणि निहिता नेङ्गयन्ति तुरीयं वाचो मनुष्या वदन्ति ॥

— *Ṛgveda*, 1.164.45

In fact, the *Ṛk* itself is unknown; for the one that we know is only a part of the larger *Ṛk* which remains hidden: "All the Gods dwell in the *Ṛk* which itself resides in the highest region of heaven."[6]

According to the Jewish mystic tradition too, God has a secret Name which "has not been sent into the world".

What do these statements mean? Are they examples of bad thought, vague and obscurantist? Or are they mere poetic images, ornamental figures of speech? Or are they trying to convey something which they find it difficult to do? And if there is some truth in them, can it not be said somewhat more analytically or, at least, without lisping?

II

If we ponder over the problem a little, we shall realize that the above statements are eminently just. If we come to think of it, we hardly know much of anything. Our world, our life, our Spirit remain shrouded in mystery. Of the world, we know only its outer forms and workings, touches and contacts; of the mind, we know only its surface layers, its pains and sensations, desires and regrets and, in some measure, even its thoughts and hopes and elations. And of the life of being, we neither know "its form, nor its end, nor its origin, nor its resting place",[7] as the *Gitā* says. If this is true generally of all life and spirit, why should speech, one of their most important expressions, be an exception?

Secondly, this approach to speech agrees with the larger approach of Indian thought. This thought conceives Reality not merely horizontally but also vertically. In this thought, Reality exists at various levels of subtlety, the gross derived from the subtle. It is like a seed containing the tree and the tree becoming the seed again. It is like a point having no dimension of its own but moving out in everwidening circles. It is like one sheath within

---

[6]ऋचो अक्षरे परमे व्योमन् यस्मिन् देवा अधि विश्वे निषेदुः।
यस्तन्न वेद किमृचा करिस्यति इत् तद् विदुस्त इमे समासते॥
— *Ṛgveda*, 1.164.39

[7]न रूपमस्येह तथोपलभ्यते नान्तो न आदिर्न च संप्रतिष्ठा।
— *Bhagvadgītā*, 15.3

another sheath. Here all actions and interactions take place at the surface and circumference but it is all quiet inside. Nonetheless, the inside is not just nothing; it holds all the seed-power and provides all the patterns, potencies and possibilities.

The word too is conceived after the above image. Viewed from one angle, it is the outermost thing; viewed from another, it is the very core of man's experience. It resides in the heart surrounded by rings of lightning and fire. There it sits darkling and pregnant, full of riddle and meaning and creation.

According to this view, words include all the worlds and planes of existence, all the levels of experience. They are carriers of man's inner life. Therefore, they are as matter-of-fact as the earth but they also wing as high as the sky. In somewhat more analytic language, one could say that a word has several layers of meanings, the deeper layers remaining hidden from the surface mind.

A word could be said to have three bodies, one inside the other. These could be called: physical, subtle, and causal. In the first reside the more dominant and direct physical meanings of a word. In this sheath, we could also include the many secondary, satellite meanings. These have their importance but they could still be regarded as the extensions of the physical meanings. These meanings are within easy reach of ordinary minds.

The subtle body contains many seed-meanings which are psychological and psychic in character. Here the word pulsates with a new life and shines with a great inner intelligence. Here the meanings are not entirely out of reach and they are revealed to a reflective mind.

The third sheath is the subtlest and it contains noumenal meanings which also support all the phenomenal meanings of a word, mental or physical. It holds the imperative seed which renews the word continually; which is self-same through all its bodily changes. This is the highest status of a word and it remains invisible. Its summit or core is hidden in the heart; which means that its meanings are not revealed to the sensuous and reasoning mind but they are accessible to the intuitive mind. It is what the *Ṛgveda* means when it says; "One man indeed seeing speech has not seen her; another hearing her has not heard her; but to another she delivers her person as a loving wife well-attired presents herself to her husband."[8]

III

In Indian thought, the word has been studied from two main angles: as sound, *śabda*, and also as object to which that sound refers, *artha*. In both cases, investigation led to underlying, hidden depths and layers. We have found how gross objects to which words refer at one level of seeing, turn into abstract forms, into luminous forms at another level of seeing, till they become thoughts, intelligences, and truths of the Spirit.

We find the same thing when we study the word as sound. It exists, as we have seen, on several levels like *vaikharī, madhyamā, paśyantī.*

Vaikharī is the spoken word, the one produced in the mouth, the one we know best in our ordinary consciousness.

In madhyamā, the word becomes mental. This status of the word cannot be perceived by the external mind but it can be apprehended by the inner mind. Also, here, the sounds of a word do not have the same sequence as we ordinarily know. They are held together in one instance as it were.

Paśyantī is essentially a conscious principle. It is a soul residing in the body of a word as a knower and a shaper.

There are other differences too. At the level of *paśyantī,* there is no difference between the denoter and the denoted—they become one; at the level of *madhyamā,* the differences remain indistinct; in *vaikharī,* they are fully perceived—here words become signs and labels as we know them.

But whatever the path of investigation we choose, they converge. Whether we start with the sound of a word or its object, both soon meet and become thought, become principles of

---

[8]उत त्वः पश्यन् न ददर्श वाचमुत त्वः श्रृण्वन् न श्रृणोत्येनाम्।
उतो त्वमस्मै तन्वं वि सस्रे जायेव पत्य उशती सुवासाः ॥
— *Ṛgveda*, 10.71.4

consciousness. To begin with, at the surface level, the sound is spoken or vocal and the meaning is physical and sensuous; and the link between the two is external and conventional. But as we go deeper and reach subtler levels, the link becomes intrinsic, the subtle in the sound responding to the subtle in the object, both being self-formations of the same mind-stuff.

It seems that the Greeks too held similar thoughts on this subject. The Greek word 'logos' is not used in the grammatical sense of a mere name of a thing or an act, That meaning was indicated by another word like 'onoma'. 'Logos', on the other hand, means the outward form by which the inward thought is expressed and also the inward thought itself. So it includes both *oratio* as well as *ratio.* Oratio is that which is spoken; ratio is the power of the mind that is manifested in speech, the *reason.* So a word is a sound which at bottom is thought.

The Greeks also made a distinction between a word that is merely uttered and the one which is made good. So a true word is also will.

IV

Thus the meanings of a word live in the spirit, in its different organs and instruments, in *buddhi*, *manas*, *prāṇa*, at different levels of their purity-states. They live as images, as concepts, as thoughts, as archetype, as Names of Gods within, as powers and attributes of the Self.

Lofty meanings live in the higher mind. In this sense, words have a meaning beyond the commonplace experiences of a man. But no one may take more out of them than he puts into them. His language is equal to his mind and experience.

In this sense, a language is made by the people who speak it. The American language, for example, is smart, racy, scintillating, animated, and brilliant but somewhat shallow. This is the ethos it has received from its writers and journalists.

Nor can the language of a nation rise above the vision and purity of its poets and thinkers. Shakespeare gave the English language power and eloquence. He made it expressive and self-reflective. Through him, one could not only express one's hates and loves and other passions better but he could also reflect on them better. The bard of the English language used no more than 10,000 different words, yet he created a great world of beauty, charm, wonder and magic, and expressed and revealed a whole gamut of human feelings, moods, emotions, hopes and despair, motives and urges, and reflected on the meaning and purpose of life in a grand style.

The Bible has helped to raise the English language morally and spiritually.

Most of the Indian languages are deep and rich. Except in certain neglected areas, even a most gifted person will not have much to contribute to them in a real way. But even the richest language needs constant airing and ventilating. This the great Tagore did for the Bengali language. He also saved it from a certain rigidity, pedantry and pompousness that had temporarily overtaken it. He brought to the doors of the common man the beauty and cadence of the Begali language as developed by Bauls and Vaishnava saints and singers.

Gandhi was no litterateur in the accepted sense of the term but he had brought with him the offerings of a pure heart that are most acceptable to Sarasvatī, the Goddess of Speech. He brought with him the homage of a life of sacrifice, the homage of a true, sincere seeking. This is the fare on which Gods in the soul live and thrive. Therefore, words revealed more to Gandhi and he contributed more to them.

This point needs making because we think erroneously that a language lives by its grammarians, pen-pushers, journalists, writers and poets in the ordinary sense. No. A language lives through its men of truth, vision, seeking and austerity even though they may not write a single sentence or compose a single line.

Chandidas and Tulasidas revealed new worlds of love, devotion and purity. Words in them shine with light and throb with life. They move a reader, melt him, transport him, awaken him, purify him, exalt him, remake him.

In Vyāsa, the language became deep like the ocean. He released all the imprisoned splendour of all the words in all the languages as it were and in him they touch the highest they are capable of. They inhabit a celestial region and are bathed in light and express their inherent sublimity. They vibrate with an inner compelling power. In him, they become revelatory, veritable mantras. To read the *Mahābhārata* is an act of deep meditation.

V

We now come to the next question: How to unlock the higher meanings?

The answer is already implied in the foregoing discussion. If higher meanings reside in the deeper layers of the mind, then they can be revealed by invoking those layers. This can be done by cultivating purity, dedication and aspiration.

"The wise reach the path of Speech by Sacrifice," declare the Vedas.[9] What is this path of sacrifice? This is the path of adoration, worship, holiness, self-giving, universality, wisdom, the path of the shedding of the lower life and its impulses.

A language is divine in origin. But it has been debased. Words have been used in the context of ambition, vulgarity, sensuality, egoistic self-aggrandizement. As a result they have picked up lower associations and connotations. These exert a downward pull and it becomes difficult to break away from their orbit. The words tend to lose their higher rhythm, resonance and vibrations. They fail to convey the larger message they carry. Therefore, words that are filled with a grand inner eloquence become spiritually dumb. But they can be restored to their original status by a life of purity, truth and wisdom.

A word conceals its meanings and powers within, hidden behind many outer coverings. Remove the wrappings; remove the husk and find the golden corn within. As the word is made pure, as

---

[9]यज्ञेन वाचः पदवीयमायन् तामन्वविन्दन्नृषिषु प्रविष्टाम् ।

— *Ṛgveda*, 10.71.3

it penetrates its outer sheaths, as it is shorn of its images, noises and echoes, it merges into thought and thought merges into silence. And what the word initially concealed, it begins to reveal. It becomes revelatory.

The Yogas use the method of concentration and meditation for entering into the larger meanings of a word, for penetrating its outer coverings. Meditation consists in turning away from the outward appearances of objects to their underlying luminous forms, and then to their deeper sources in the mind. But in this journey, it does not reject the outward forms altogether. In fact, that is not possible. Instead, it makes them its starting-point and puts them to a new use and gives them a new treatment. It gives them *continued attention.*

The ordinary mind is distracted and dispersed. Therefore, the knowledge of the object it reflects is also obscure and dim, its existence diluted. The attention shifts continuously and one *rūpa* (form) is replaced by another. But when the mind learns to linger on its object for some length of time, it itself acquires self-concentration. It becomes joyous and luminous and it lends these qualities to its object. The ordinary mind receives its object from outside as it were. But the new *rūpa* of a concentrated mind derives its elements from those that are already in the mind.

As meditation deepens, even luminous *rūpa* is left behind and we make our acquaintance with its source in the mind. We now enter the world of *nāma*, of *vijñāna,* of mind. Here there is only one reality, the reality of a universal mind. Beyond this lies the realm of the Spirit.

Meditation brings interiorization. Behind gross forms, we begin to see luminous forms; behind luminous forms, figures of Godhead. The sensuous and *manas*-experiences become ideas of the mind, become categories of the intellect, become images and powers of the psyche, become attributes of the Self, become Names of Gods, become Names of the Name. The concrete becomes the vehicle of the abstract; the many are interpenetrated by the One. The manifest reveals the Unmanifest.

This point needs pondering over. For it explains how to an inward look, even physical objects become truths of being, abodes of Gods; while to the outward mind, even Gods become only physical objects and acquire merely utilitarian meanings.

VI

Let us anticipate somewhat and take by way of illustration 'fire', also a great God in the Vedic pantheon. When we meditate on this word, it acquires increasingly deeper and richer meanings. Ordinary perception reveals only its physical forms and attributes; but to a deepened sensibility, these forms and attributes become emotional and intellectual. And yet, these too are rooted in the psychic and the spiritual. Under the concentrated power of mind, under the searchlight of meditation, fire reveals its *tanmātrā*, its, *mahat*-form, and even its *avyakta*-form. It also becomes a power of the Spirit.

As we meditate on it, the ordinary fire that we know disappears. In its place is revealed its more subtle and luminous form. Then even that disappears and in its place is revealed its more universal aspect. We realize that not only does fire inhabit our hearth and home and cook our food, it also resides in our digestion; it also shines in our intelligence. It is also the energy behind our spiritual labours. Not only does it illumine our path, it is also one with the light of the eye and the Sun. It reveals its divinity too. It is both Gods as well as their messenger. It invokes Gods; it is Gods. It also burns in the soul as aspiration for Gods.

This knowledge which is revealed is not ordinary knowledge. It is intimate knowledge. It wells up from within. In this knowledge, one becomes a part of it. When one knows that fire burns, it is knowledge of the mind; but when it burns him, it becomes direct knowledge. It becomes knowledge of the heart. The Vedic Rishis worshipped this Fire which burns up all impurities, only the Pure remaining. Not without reason does the word fire derive from a Sanskrit root *pū*, which means to purify.

What fire inspired in the fire-worshippers, the sky inspired in the sky-worshippers. In the ordinary view, the sky refers to an outside phenomenon, or to its mental image at the best. From a realistic viewpoint, this image is a very inadequate representation of the sky even if we were to accept the representational theory of reality. But as we turn our concentrated attention on it, the sensuous image begins to yield to psychic meanings. It becomes a vehicle of the greater life of the mind. It becomes the symbol of infinity, pervasiveness, wonder, freedom, irresistibility. It becomes a power of the soul. It becomes an attribute of the Godhead. The sky is *ananta*, endless, but it supports all beginnings and all ends. It is formless but it supports all forms. The infinity of the sky is only a facet of the infinity of the mind which itself derives from the infinity of the Spirit. It reconciles all contradictions. Itself unmoving, it is swifter than mind. It moves, it moves not. It is far, it is near. It is within, it is without.

The sky has been a great object of worship in many religious traditions. With its psychic attributes, it enters into the four *samāpattis* of Buddhist Yoga, which are very advanced stages of meditation. Contemplation on the sky is repeatedly mentioned in the Upanishads. According to some, the very word contemplation derives from the practice of observing a marked space, *templum*, in the sky. According to the Pātañjala Yoga, the still posture of the Yogi is won by meditating on the *ananta*, the endless, the sky.

One could also choose non-material objects for meditation. Buddha chose the widely common experience of suffering or pain. Man knows suffering generally in its outer manifestation as mere pain and distress; he also thinks he can cure it by satisfying his desires; he further thinks it has been imposed on him wrongly and from outside. But by meditation, the word acquires increasingly deeper meanings. The suffering is no longer personal. One begins to see the suffering of others in one's own suffering; he also suffers in the suffering of others. Suffering is also no longer experienced as an isolated instance; in that instance, one sees all suffering, past, present, and future. One sees the law of suffering. One sees in it the source from which it arises, the whole chain of which it is only a part.

One also sees in suffering another meaning—the meaning of suffering endured willingly and borne cheerfully. One learns from it the lesson of indifference—indifference not only to what is called pain but also to that which is known as pleasure. In this indifference, one also finds the message of a higher joy, the message of deliverance and freedom.

In the same way, the meanings are increasingly deepened if we meditate on such moral and spiritual truths as non-violence (*ahiṃsā*), truth (*satya*), non-stealing (*asteya*), celibacy (*brahmacarya*), non-possession (*aparigraha*), purity (*śauca*), compassion (*karuṇā*), right livelihood (*samyak ājīvikā*), and right exertion (*samyak vyāyāma*). In fact, these values need meditating upon if they are to yield their larger, inner truths and rise above their ordinary, egoistic meanings.

VII

One could also choose for meditation some psychic truth embodied in one of the Names or Forms or Aspects or Incarnations of God. Names of Rama and Krishna are two such popular choices in India. Let us see, for the sake of illustration, how it works.

Suppose Krishna is your chosen deity and you aspire to enter into His Spirit and know the deeper meanings of His Name. Then, first, with open eyes, watch this word in action; watch its contexts and its uses. Read Krishna's life; listen to His deeds and teachings; study the stories, tales and myths around Him. That will help you to make contact with various shades and meanings that go into the making of the name, Krishna. This in turn will help you to contact Krishna on the psychic plane.

During all this while, reflect and meditate on the Name and Form of Krishna. In this way, deeper meanings and vibrations will begin to unravel themselves. A silent process of deeper understanding will start within you.

Thus we see that *svādhyāya, śravaṇa, kīrtana,* or the study of scriptures, listening to and singing God's names and glories are necessary parts of meditation. They help it. Mind and senses enrich each other. God's glories are both sensuous, and mental as well as spiritual. They reside both on the earth as well as in heaven.

After some practice and with the help of the above aids, when the mind conquers its own vagaries to some extent and is somewhat steadied and is in a position to turn its gaze within, it acquires a capacity for contemplating on the name. It begins to receive different vibrations that go into the making of this name; it begins to realize the appropriateness and justice of this name. The deity is called *Kṛṣṇa* (popular spellings 'Krishna') because He draws (*kṛṣ*) unto Himself His devotees; or, because He overpowers all; or, because He bends the wicked and the unrighteous like a bow; or, because He swallows everything at the time of the great deluge.

The deepening meditation will also yield other Names of the same Name. The mind realizes that *Kṛṣṇa* is rightly called *Viṣṇu* because He surpasses (*viṣ*) all, overcomes all, prevades all, is the destination of all. He is called *Hari* because He steals away (*hṛ*) the hearts of His worshippers; or, takes away their sins; or, carries away His portion of man's oblations and offerings. He is the resting place (*dhāma*) of the Law and the Truth; therefore, He is also called *Ṛtadhāman*. He always abides in His true nature (*sattva)*; therefore, He is called *Sāttvata*. He never lapses (*cu*) from His true Being; therefore, He is called *Acyuta*. His understanding and energy never dull or blunt (*kuṇṭha*); therefore, He is known as *Vaikuṇṭha*. He is called *Aja* because He is unborn.

Because spiritual aspirants attain to Him through self-control (*dama*), He is called *Dāmodara*. He saves the world or the Earth (*gām)* from sinking; therefore, He is called *Govinda*. The rays of the Sun and the Moon and the Fires are His hair (*keśa*); therefore, He is called *Keśava*. He is the Lord of man's five senses (*hṛṣīka*); therefore, He is called *Hṛṣīkeśa*. He bestows delight (*harṣa*) on all; therefore, He is called *Hṛṣi*. He is the dwelling-place (*vāsa)* of all creatures; therefore, He is also called *Vāsudeva*. He is the womb (*garbha*) of the Vedas, of all the light of Knowledge, and of all the waters (*pṛśni*) of Immortality; therefore, He is called *Pṛśigarbha*. He is called *Bhagvān*, because He is invested with all glory, grace, radiance, beauty, bounty, dignity, prosperity, happiness, splendour and auspiciousness (*bhaga*); or, because He destroys (*bhañj*) all sorrows, sins, evils and delusions; or, because He practises (*bhaj*) truth, meditation and austerity; or, because He has preached *Dharma* integrally and also separately (*vibhakta*) in its manifoldness (*bhāga*).

VIII

These are some of the examples to show how meditation helps in unlocking the higher meanings of the words. Meditation is a great key for opening up the deeper meanings of moral and spiritual truths. Whether one meditates on physical elements or directly on moral and psychic truths, the results are the same. For the two paths meet and soon both become truths of the Spirit.

Part Two

CHAPTER 9

Vedic Gods: Concrete Images

Higher meanings become names of the powers of the psyche, names of the Gods within, names of the attributes of the Self. These meanings are the true objects of religious groping and the mystic quest. These meanings are already placed in the soul but they have to be rediscovered by love and sacrifice. On the terrestrial plane, the path to Self-discovery lies through world-discovery.

In the light of the preceding discussion, it would be interesting to turn to Hindu religious thought, particularly to its ancient Vedic expression, and find out how it embodies these meanings and how it mirrors the higher quest and the higher life; and whether it has still some specific characteristics, even though it follows general laws of the mind and the heart.

Such a study will be useful in more than one way. Firstly, it will help to complete our investigation into higher meanings. Secondly, it will add to our understanding of Hinduism, one of the most ancient and still one of the major world-religions. Thirdly, it will throw light on the ancient Gods of many Asian and European countries, Gods by now so completely forgotten that we cannot study them directly; but perhaps we can do that indirectly through Hindu Gods.

There was a time when these Gods satisfied the religious urges of their devotees. But in the course of time they came under attack from new Gods that were appearing on the horizon. They are by now completely replaced but the old persecution still continues though in a modified form. The new persecutors are not theologians and religious zealots but staid academicians. To them these Gods are not false but primitive. They hold that these Gods represented the attempt of the primitive mind to express, however imperfectly, through Nature's symbols and objects, its groping for a unitary principle. At this stage of human evolution, it was difficult for man's mind to rise above the sensuous to the intellectual and the spiritual, and from the many to the one. That was left for a later generation to achieve, reaching its high water-mark in Christianity and modern Europe.

If Gods are born of religious urges and spiritual intuitions, it is difficult to see how modern European Christians are superior in this respect and, therefore, how their 'one God' could be truer than the 'many Gods' of their ancestors.

A look at the Hindu Gods may throw light on this aspect of the subject. The Hindu pantheon has changed to some extent but the old Gods are still active and are still undertstood though under modified names. Hindu India has a sense of continuity with its past which other nations that changed their religions at some later stage, lack. It is also known that the Hindu religion preserves many old layers and forms. Therefore, its study may link us not only with its own past forms but also with the religious consciousness, intuitions and forms that prevailed in the past in Europe, in Greece, in Rome, in many Scandinavian and Baltic countries, amongst the Germanic and Slavic peoples and also in several countries of the Middle East. In short, the study may reveal a fundamental form of spiritual consciousness which is wider than its Hindu expression.

II

If we look at the word 'God', we find that though today it has acquired a forced, intellectualized, outward meaning appropriate to the mentality of the present age, yet it still retains the memory of the idea of a deity of a more intuitive people and of more spontaneous times.

Etymologists connect this word with Gothic *guth*, which is Skt. *huta*, which means 'one to whom oblations are made' and, therefore, one who is worshipped. It connects us with the period when fire was a great living symbol of the deity within and around. In later times, the symbol was denounced as nature-worship by some sects but there was a time when it claimed, along with the Sun and the Sky, universal acceptance. Even Moses who belonged to an iconoclastic tradition had a glimpse of his God through the medium of fire. And in the Old Testament itself, certain hymns are considered 'nature hymns' by its scholars.

Etymologists also connect the word with the German word *gotse* whose original meaning was an image or a figure. In the Norse language also, the word meant 'image of a deity'. So the word perhaps referred to the practice of worshipping God through various images and figures, a practice quite common amongst different peoples all over the world, ancient as well as modern.

There is another feature worth noticing. Spengler[1] tells us that the old German word for God "was a neutral plural and was turned into a masculine singular by Christian propaganda". The same is true of the word in the Norse and Teutonic languages. But after the heathens were converted, God changed his gender and number. This can hardly be regarded as the deepening of its meaning and conception.

The Hebrew word *Elohim* too is plural in origin, form and sense. The same is true of the Semitic word *El.* It is not the name of a deity common to all but is a common name for different deities in the Semitic world.

Thus we see that the untutored and the more spontaneous intuition of the human race excludes neither the plurality of Gods nor the use of images and nature symbols from its religious sensibility. The denial comes when the mind becomes too conceptual; or when dogmatic faith develops faster than understanding. But there is also a spiritual motive to the denial to which we shall turn later on.

III

If we study the ancient religious literature of the Hindus, particularly the Vedas, the Upanishads and the *Mahābhārata*,

---

[1]Oswald Spengler, *The Hour of Decision*, London, 1934, p. 311.

certain things stand out prominently. The very first thing is a very large use of concrete images. There are Gods like Indra, Pūṣaṇa, Varuṇa, Aśvins for whom there are no physical correspondences, but many important Gods like Sūrya, Agni, Marut take their names after natural objects.

There is also another important feature that we notice. The spiritual consciousness of the race is expressed in terms of the plurality of Gods. In these two respects, at least, the Hindu approach agreed with the spiritual intuition of other ancient peoples.

We have already seen that the physical and the intellectual are not opposed to one another. The names of physical objects become names of ideas, names of psychic truths, names of Gods; sensuous truths become intellectual truths, become spiritual truths.

As the knowledge of the senses becomes the knowledge of the *manas* and the *buddhi*, the knowledge originating in the higher organs of the mind also tends to filter down to the levels of the *manas* and the senses. So in this way even the highest knowledge has its form, colour and sound. This need not lower down its quality in any way. In fact, this is the only way in which the sense-bound mind understands something of the higher knowledge.

This reverberating, echoing and imaging takes place up and down the whole corridor of the mind at all levels of abstraction. Here, as we traverse the path, we meet physical-forms, sound-forms, vision-forms, thought-forms, universal-forms, all echoes of each other. We meet *mantras* and *yantras* and icons of various efficacies and psychic qualities. In one sense, they are not the light above but they are its important formations. They invoke the celestial and raise up the terrestrial.

So the names of even the most concrete things have a meaning larger than their immediate referents. There is nothing, however lowly, which does not yield these meanings. Here stones sermonize and every brook is a book of learning. Here birds and animals teach wisdom. A small passage in the Old Testament (Proverbs, 30) uses the figures of a leech, an eagle, a serpent, a locust, an ant, a spider, a lion, a greyhound, a goat, to illustrate certain truths of life. To the author of this *Proverb*, the way of a man with a maid is like the way of an eagle in the air, or the way of a serpent upon the rock, or the way of a ship in the midst of the sea. Here the author is not saying anything about the eagle or the serpent; he is using these figures in order to say something about man himself.

Similarly, in the Vedas, words like the horse or the cow have larger meanings. In these meanings, they become names of the boons which the worshippers seek from their Gods; they even enter into the epithets of these Gods. For example, the word for a horse in the Vedas is *vāja*. It derives from the root *vaj* or *uj*, which also gives us words like *ugra* (mighty, strong, terrible), *vajra* (hard and mighty; it is also the name of Indra's celebrated weapon with which he reduces his foes), and *ojas* (strength, vigour). So the word stands not only for the horse but also for the strength, speed and impetuosity of a horse, and for the general ideas of power, energy, swiftness, heroism, virility and invincibility in war. These the devotee seeks as boons from his Gods.

The word also came to mean battle, a contest and, by an extended use, the booty of a battle or the prize of a contest. In composition, we also got words like *vājapeya*, the drink of strength and battle, and *vājinīvat*, rich in horses. Words like *vājinīvasu* (bestowing strength and power), *vājadā* or *vājadāvan* (bestowing vigour, speed, wealth and prizes) also became epithets of Gods. Agni, the Fire-God, is *vājapati*, the lord of booty and reward.

In the same way and by the same process, familiar objects like the Sun, the Moon, the Sky assumed divine forms. They expressed the light, the power, the grandeur, the beauty, the freedom, the joy, and the law of the Spirit. The figure of human love was used to express the depth and intimacy of divine love and the purity of the latter was used to transform human love.

Thus the use of physical images in no way limits the presentation of the most abstract truths. This is best illustrated by the Upanishads which discuss the most abstract subjects in the most concrete images. Here, the Person in the yonder Sun is the same as the Person in the Eye. Here the figures of the sun, the moon, the quarters of heaven, the atmosphere, the waters, the fire, the lightning, man's five breaths, even his eyes, ears, nose, hands and legs are used to lead to the most secret truths. Here one image is used to suggest another and both to suggest the imageless; here, a negative points to a positive and vice versa, and both point to a Reality which is beyond duality.

There is another reason why images in the Vedas and the Upanishads are concrete. When the fever of the soul subsides, when the mind becomes calm, when the spiritual consciousness opens, things are no longer lifeless. In this state, things which have hitherto been regarded as ordinary are full of life, light, and consciousness. In this state, "the earth meditates as it were; water meditates as it were; mountains meditate as it were".[2] In this state, no need is felt to separate the abstract from the concrete because both are eloquent with the same message, because both image one another. In this state, everything expresses the divine; everything is the seat of the divine; everything is That; mountains, rivers and the great earth are but the Tathāgata, as a Chinese teacher, Hsu Yun, proclaimed after his spiritual awakening.

IV

In an age and amongst the people in whom the spiritual consciousness is alive, the world and words are also alive. They are not what they appear to the surface mind. They point to something deep and beyond. They incarnate profound truths of the self. But when spiritual consciousness is withdrawn and a physical consciousness comes to the fore, objects and words too become dead and self-contained. They no longer convey anything beyond their most outward, physical meanings. They become dumb.

A study of languages from this viewpoint would be very interesting. It would show how a spiritual age or mentality puts

---

[2]*Chāndogya Upaniṣad*, 7.6.1.

forth words and names and uses them in senses which are no longer understood by a more materialist age or utilitarian mentality. The same old words are there but they do not mean the same things; the old scriptures are there but the light goes out of them. The new age deals with shells only. And the hiatus is not linguistic but mental. Objects and words exist at various levels. To a physical consciousness, they yield only physical and outward meanings.

This explains the sad plight of many pioneer Indologists and Vedic scholars. They were competent grammarians and linguists and did useful work but their own share of the harvest was husk and straw.

This discussion throws light on another point too. There is a school of thought which says that the Vedas and the Upanishads contain secret teachings, that the sages secured this secrecy by using words having double and treble meanings in order to hide the true teachings from the merely curious and the idle.

We too believe that the teachings are secret but the secrecy is unintended. The secrecy is in the nature of things. As we have seen, words have multiple meanings and the higher meanings remain hidden. And there is no way of revealing them unless one's life is purified and one's consciousness is raised up.

So there is no planned secrecy, and no linguistic trick to secure it. There is no code of human devising and the knowledge of the Vedas would not become available if the code were broken by some scholarly method. The path to their knowledge is the path of love and sacrifice. But this is a difficult path and mostly remains untrodden and thus the higher meanings are successfully hidden.

Not only hidden but also easily confused with lower meanings and outer symbols. The soul employs outer symbols to convey inner realities. In fact, all true meanings lie in the soul and the outward symbols and names are merely their channels and vehicles. The soul uses them for its own self-discovery. It refers to them but is not limited by them.

Every word, truth and experience is self-transcending. In

everything that is spoken, there is the unspoken; in everything known, there is the unknown. The soul offers worship and homage to this transcendental, this unspoken, this unknown.

The Vedic seers made this distinction quite clear. In all the visible signs they used, they saw the invisible. "He who has drunk thinks that the herb which men crush is the Soma; but of him whom Brahmans truly know as Soma no one truly tastes,"[3] they declared of Soma—the intoxicating herb to a physical mind but a veritable deity to a spiritual consciousness. This deity, this embodiment of the joy of existence, "is sheltered by religious vows, guarded by *bṛhatī* hymns"; it even "stands listening to the stones that crush it; but none tastes of it who dwells on earth,"[4] the Vedas add. The true, kingly Soma was found by the resplendent Pūṣaṇa concealed in the cave of the heart, *guhāhitam.*[5]

The God Agni too is not the ordinary fire. In fact, to the seers, the ordinary fire derives from the Transcendental Fire and not the other way round. Vatsapri, the Vedic sage, says, "Agni was first born above the sky, *divaspari*; as *jātavedāḥ,* he was born the second time amongst us; the friend of man, he was born the third time in the waters; the sage kindling him eternally praises him."[6]

The same sage cryptically says, "We recognize thy threefold stations, O Agni, and thy three forms; we recognize the many stations occupied by thee; we know what thy supreme secret appellation is, *nāma parmaṃ guhā;* we know thy source (*dhāma*), from where thou have proceeded."[7]

---

[3]सोमं मन्यते पपिवान् यत् संपिषन्त्योषधिम्।
सोमं यं ब्रह्माणो विदुर्न तस्याश्नाति कश्चन॥
— *Ṛgveda*, 10.85.3

[4]आच्छद्विधानैर्गुपितो वार्हतैः सोम रक्षितः।
ग्राव्णामिच्छृण्वन् तिष्ठसि न ते अश्नाति पार्थिवः॥
— *Ṛgveda*, 10.85.4

[5]पूषा राजानमाघृणिरपगूढं गुहा हितम्। अविन्दच्चित्रबर्हिषम्॥
— *Ṛgveda*, 1.23.14.

[6]दिवस्परि प्रथमं जज्ञे अग्निरस्मद् द्वितीयं परि जातवेदाः।
तृतीयमप्सु नृमणा अजस्रमिन्धान एनं जरतेः स्वाधीः॥
— *Ṛgveda*, 10.45.1

[7]विद्मा ते अग्ने त्रेधा त्रयाणि विद्मा ते धाम विभृता पुरुत्रा।
विद्मा ते नाम परमं गुहा यद्विद्मा तमुत्सं यत् आजगन्थ॥
— *Ṛgveda*, 10.45.2

This is a most secret knowledge, this knowledge about Agni's true abode and forms and appellations. This is revealed only to the pure. True Fire is to be seen in the cave of the heart, to put it in the Upanishadic language; the same was also known by latter-day saints like Kabir as *gagana-guphā*, the sky-cave, where the Deity, the Secret Name, *satnāma*, dwells.

CHAPTER 10

Names of Gods: Vedic

We have seen that the Vedas make large use of concrete images in the presentation of their Gods. They also insist that, in some sense, these Gods are not fully known; that what our heart worships is not the same as what our eyes see and what our ears hear.

There is also another distinctive feature—all Gods have multiple names. And the knowledge of these names, as in the case of the appellations of Agni, is an important knowledge. It is also a holy knowledge.

In all spiritual traditions, there is something analogous to it. The God of the Jews has many names. He is *Bore Olam* (creator of the world), *Kedosh Yisrael* (Holy One of Israel), *Ho-Malkom* (the Omnipresent Place), *El-Elion* (the Most High One), *En Sof* (the Infinite One). But according to Jewish mysticism, God has also a secret name which should not even be uttered. Therefore, the Jews simply called it "the Great Name", or "the Great, Precious Name", or just "the Name". This name was considered so secret that it was told only to the initiates and the pious and that too in whispers so that it was not overheard by the laity.[1]

Islam too admits of God's Names though it denies His Forms. But the admission receives a certain narrowing at the hands of the

---

[1]This most secret Name was rendered by four letters YHWH. But as a result of this secrecy, no one knows how it was pronounced. Its present rendering 'Jehovah' appeared for the first time as late as 1516 in Christian texts and is regarded as simply incorrect by competent authorities. When religious men referred to this most secret Name, they used substitutes and even the substitutes were substituted. For example, they said *Adoshem* in the place of *Adonai* and *Elokhim* in the place of *Elohim*.

more orthodox and faithful. For a Name to be valid, it must be confirmed by the Quran. God is *Ash-Shafi*, the healer, but not *At-Tabib*, the physician, for the Quran does not use the latter epithet. Similarly, the Arabic *Allah* is to be preferred to the Persian *Khudā* though both may mean the same thing. Naturally, in this kind of approach, there is no place for names like Jupiter, Brahma, or Īśvara, for they derive from the languages of the *kāfirs* (infidels).

Socrates presents this idea in the language of understanding. He proclaims the awe, mystery and unknowability of Gods and their names but also tells us how these are ultimately the names of man's own intentions and meanings. He says, "Of the Gods we know nothing, either of their natures or of the names by which they call themselves... Let us, then, if you please, in the first place announce to them that we are not enquiring about them; we do not presume that we are able to do so; but we are enquiring about the meaning of men in giving them these names."[2]

According to Hindu thought too, the names of Gods are not names of external beings. These are names of the truths of man's own highest Self. So the knowledge of the epithets of Gods is a form of self-knowledge. Gods and their names embody truths of the deeper Spirit and meditation on them in turn invokes those truths. But those truths are many and, therefore, Gods and their names too are many, though they are all held together in the unity of a spiritual consciousness. In this chapter, we shall make our acquaintance with some of the names of some of the Vedic Gods.

II

Nature's mighty phenomena like the earth, the sky, the sun and the stars are not only Gods but each one of them also bears several names. The famous *Amarakośa* gives 36 names for Fire, 27 names for the Sun, 12 names for Sun's rays, 29 names for Water, 20 names for Wind, 11 names for Night. The list is partial.

The reasons for giving many names for a single object are easy to follow. The modern man is in a hurry to communicate as much

---

[2] *Cratylus*, p. 401.

as he understands of a thing. So one or two names to indicate it are sufficient for his purpose. But the old sages were in no such haste. They saw in familiar objects like the earth and the sun more than our age does. They saw in them sources and springs of their own lives. They saw that these things were part of one Great Life; that they were meeting-points of great spiritual truths; that they were images, symbols and signs of great and mighty forces; that they revealed what was concealed; that they prefigured a mighty design; that they were kith and kin, friends and lovers. But in order to yield their deeper meanings, they demanded continued fellowship. This the old sages gave ungrudgingly and joyfully. This filled their hearts and the fullness of their hearts broke out in songs of praise.

No wonder, these seers had to have several names to signify the inner and larger life of these objects. These men were not reporters, communicators of outer information about indifferent things. They were worshippers and lovers. They were singers of a larger life, of a deeper fellowship, of a beauty, grandeur and bounty beyond the reach of mere senses and imagination.

So they had scores of names for the Earth. To the modern man, the earth means soil, dry land, cultivable land or at best the globe on which we live. But to the ancients, it was very much more than that. Therefore, they had many names to bring out its innerness. They call it the unmoving one, *acalā*; the stable one, *sthirā*; the boundless one, *anantā*; the seat of all saps and flavours, *rasā*; the spacious one, *urvī*; the great one, *mahī*; the broad and extended one, *pṛthvī* or *pṛthivī*; the wide one, *vipulā*; the first one, *ādyā*; one holding all treasures, *vasumatī* or *vasuṃdharā* or *vasudhā*; one granting rightly and liberally, *ṛju-vani* and *ṛju-hastā;* the bearer of all beings, *jagadvahā*; the great nurse, *dhātrī*; one supporting or holding all, *dharaṇī*; the mother, *mātā*; the all-enduring or the patient one, *kṣmā* or *kṣamā* or *sahā* or *sarvasahā*; the crop-yielding or the fertile one, *urvarā*.

Similarly, the Sun too is given many names. He is called the bright one, *bhānu,* the flaming one, *arci*, the brilliant one, *arka*; he is of variegated lustre and shines with light, *citrabhānu*; he vivifies and animates, *savitṛ* or *sūrya*; he warms and burns, *tapana*; he is gracious, majestic, excellent, a great dispenser, *bhaga*; he removes all darkness, *tamopaha*; he is the eyes of the world, *lokalocana*; he brings about all seasons and creates all time, *kālakṛta*; he appears in twelve forms or is the soul of twelve months, *dvādaśātmā;* he rides a chariot drawn by seven horses representing either the seven colours of the rainbow or the seven days of the week, *saptāśvaḥ*; like an eagle with majestic wings, he moves through the sky and is, therefore, called *suparṇa*.[3] He is the witness of man's actions and secret intentions, *karmasākṣī*. He is also called *agra-bhuj*, one who has precedence in the offered oblations.

III

Similarly, we have many names for Fire. It purifies, *pāvaka*. It is holy, brilliantly white, unsullied, *śucīḥ*. It is a living, breathing thing, *anala*, from a verbal root *an*, to breathe. It is homed in splendour, *kṛpa-nīḷa*.

Fire has flaming locks, *śociṣkeśa*; it has the wood for its womb, *kṛpīṭayoni*; its path is smoky, *kṛṣṇavartani*; it moves up serpentinely, *agni*; it is the fire of digestion, *āśayāgni*; it partakes of our offerings, *hutāśana* or *hutabhakṣa* or *hutabhuj* or *havirbhuj*; it carries our offerings to Gods or manes, *vahni*, *havyavāhana*, *kavyavāhana*; it is the mouth of all Gods and they receive our offerings through it, *sarvadeva-mukha*; it is the great dissolvent which consumes all, digests all, *pācana;* it possesses all, knows all, *jātavedas*; it burns, scorches, roasts, *dahana*; it goes up in seven tongues, *saptajihva*. Those tongues are called *kālī* (dark), *karālī* (formidable), *mano-javā* (having the speed of the mind), *sulohitā* (of beautiful red colour), *sudhumrā* (of beautiful or thick smoke), *ugrā* (impetuous), *sphulinginī* (sparkling or emitting sparks), *pradīptā* (shining).

Fire has been glorified in invoking the manes who have been

---

[3]For the same reason, the Sun God is represented with a falcon's head in the Egyptian pantheon.

called *agniṣvatta*, those whose bodies have been tasted (therefore, purified) by the funeral fire.

Many of the names we have given for fire could be derived from its physical attributes and its function in the Vedic ritual of worship; but it has also names which came directly from man's psychic being and even the physical names were used for their psychic significance. In short, to the Vedic seers, fire was a God and worshipped as such. Therefore, in the very first Sūkta of the *Ṛgveda*, praise is rendered unto Fire, the priest, *purohitam*, the divine ministrant; *devamṛtvijam*, the summoner; *hotāram*, the one who holds all treasures; *ratnadhātamam*, the radiant one; *rājantam*, the protector of sacrifices; *adhvarāṇāṃ gopām*; the illuminator of truth, *ṛtasya dīdivim*; the sovereign lord of the sacrifices, *rājantamadhvarāṇām.*

Fire is all-knowing, all-possessing, and also the lord of all men, *viśva-pati*;[4] the beloved of many, *puru-priyam.*[5] He is called wise, *kavi*;[6] young, *yuvā*, the youngest or the everyouthful, *sadā-yaviṣṭha.*[7] He is invoked by oblations of butter, *ghṛtāhavana*;[8] he is lord of the house, *gṛhapati*;[9] the observer of truth, *satyadharman*;[10] the remover of all pains, *amīvacātana*;[11] self-born, *tanūnapāt*[12] (literally, son of himself); the desire and praise of men, *narāśansa*;[13] beloved, *priya*;[14] sweet-tongued, *madhujihva*;[15] immortal, *amṛta*;[16] he is also terrible, *rudra*;[17] vast, *mahān*;[18] illimitable, *animāna*;[19] resplendent, *puruścandra*;[20] one who moves everywhere freely, *pṛthu pragāman*;[21] he is irreproachable, *anavadya*;[22] intelligent, *medhira*;[23] free from deceit or one who cannot be trifled with, *adābhya*;[24] one who defends pious acts, *vratapā*;[25] he is everywhere, *vibhū.*[26] He is our auspicious friend,

---

[4]*Ṛgveda*, 1.12.2
[5]Ibid.
[6]Ibid., 1.12.6
[7]Ibid., 1.26.2
[8]Ibid., 1.12.5
[9]Ibid., 1.12.6
[10]Ibid., 1.12.7
[11]Ibid.
[12]Ibid., 1.13.2
[13]Ibid., 1.13.3
[14]Ibid., 1.26.7
[15]Ibid., 1.13.3
[16]Ibid., 1.26.9
[17]Ibid., 1.27.10
[18]Ibid., 1.27.11
[19]Ibid.
[20]Ibid.
[21]Ibid., 1.27.2
[22]Ibid., 1.31.9
[23]Ibid., 1.31.2
[24]Ibid., 1.31.10
[25]Ibid.
[26]Ibid., 1.9.5

śivaḥ sakhā[27] and we are his kinsmen, *jāmayaḥ*.[28] He dwells in all men, *viśvacarṣaṇi*.[29] The *Ṛgveda* says that those who have Agni for their protector will have no vanquisher.[30]

IV

But there are other Gods in Vedic times and Vedic literature like Indra, Pūṣaṇa, Varuṇa, where even the semblance of a physical tethering is dropped and the symbols are purely psychic. It does not mean that all physical references are dropped. This is impossible. For one reason, because the physical and the spiritual are not wholly different. For another, because the physical is part of the language and understanding of the mind. So long as we try to understand a thing mentally and express it in language, the physical is necessary. In the Bible, there are such constant references to God's eyes, ears, feet and hands that one wonders whether one was not dealing with an anthropomorphic being, rather enlarged and glorified but still human.

This is inevitable. One could start either by having a somewhat physical or concrete symbol and then investing it with more psychic qualities; or one could start with a somewhat more abstract symbol and then give it more physical attributes. In either case, this double process of cross-reference and cross-fertilization is necessary. The physical has to be raised up; the divine has to be brought down.

Of these psychic Gods in the Vedic literature, Indra is the most celebrated one. In the *Ṛgveda*, he is called the ruler of the world, *īśāna*;[31] the celebrated, *śrutam*;[32] mighty, *mahān*;[33] powerful, *vṛṣaṇa*;[34] invincible, *astṛtam*;[35] of unbounded strength, *amitaujā*;[36] never to be defeated or always compliant, *apratiṣkuta*;[37] accomplisher of wonderful deeds, *dasma*;[38] destroyer of the city of the enemies, *purām bhinduḥ*;[39] he is wise, *vipaścitam*;[40] to him

[27]Ibid., 1.31.1
[28]Ibid., 1.31.10
[29]Ibid., 1.27.9
[30]Ibid., 1.27.8.
[31]Ibid., 1.5.10
[32]Ibid., 1.6.6
[33]Ibid., 1.63.1
[34]Ibid., 1.16.1
[35]Ibid., 1.4.4
[36]Ibid., 1.11.4
[37]Ibid., 1.7.6
[38]Ibid., 1.4.6
[39]Ibid., 1.11.4.
[40]Ibid, 1.4.4.

belongs wonderful splendour, *citra bhānu*;[41] he is lord of all wealth, *vasupati*;[42] performer of good works, *sukratu*;[43] lord of many blessings, *īśāna vāryāṇām*;[44] maker of beautiful forms or doer of good works, *surūpa kṛtnu*;[45] sustainer of all pious acts, *viśvasya karmaṇo dhartā*;[46] he is wise, *kavi*;[47] radiant as the sun, *sūracakṣas*;[48] he is master of a hundred powers or insights or counsels or he has performed a hundred sacrifices, *śatkratu*;[49] he comes hastening to us, *tūtujāna*;[50] he is mighty in battle, *vājeṣu vājina*;[51] a doer of many deeds, *vṛṣa karman*;[52] a bestower of riches, cows and light, *godā*.[53] In one single line of a Sūkta (8.81.2), he is called *tuvi kūmin*, powerful in action; *tuvi deṣṇa*, a bestower of many gifts; *tuvi magha*, lord of great wealth; *tuvi mātra,* very efficacious. He is also *tuvi nṛmṇa*,[54] very valiant; *tuvi śagma*,[55] capable of doing much; *tuvi prati*,[56] a powerful resistor; *tuvi bādha*,[57] a mighty oppressor of the enemies.

He is the giver of unfailing succour, *akṣitoti*;[58] he is ever-bounteous, *satrādāvan*.[59]

He is much praised or praised by many, *puruṣṭuta*;[60] much invoked or invoked by many, *puru-hūta*;[61] he is praised with zeal, *ariṣṭuta*;[62] he is praised by devoted men, *arigūrta*;[63] he is praised in songs, *girvāhas*[64] and celebrated in Ṛk verses, *ṛgmiyam*;[65] he is the true object of praise and he also delights in invocations, *girvaṇas*.[66]

He is everywhere, *vibhu*;[67] he is the master, *prabhu*.[68] His works are always right and honest, *ṛju-kratu*.[69]

As in the Bible, he is also given ears and eyes. He is young,

[41]Ibid., 1.3.4
[42]Ibid., 1.9.9
[43]Ibid., 1.5.6
[44]Ibid., 1.5.2
[45]Ibid., 1.4.1
[46]Ibid., 1.11.4
[47]Ibid.
[48]Ibid., 1.16.1
[49]Ibid., 1.4.9
[50]Ibid., 1.3.6
[51]Ibid., 1.4.9
[52]Ibid., 1.63.4
[53]Ibid., 1.4.2
[54]Ibid., 4.22.6
[55]Ibid., 6.44.2
[56]Ibid., 1.30.9
[57]Ibid., 1.32.6
[58]Ibid., 1.5.9
[59]Ibid., 1.7.6
[60]Ibid., 1.57.4
[61]I bid., 1.30.10
[62]Ibid., 8.1.22
[63]Ibid., 1.186.3
[64]Ibid., 1.30.5
[65]Ibid., 1.9.9
[66]Ibid., 1.5.7
[67]Ibid., 1.9.5
[68]Ibid., 1.9.5
[69]Ibid., 1.81.7

yuvā;[70] he listens attentively or he hears all things, *āśrut-karṇa*;[71] he has one thousand eyes, *sahasrākṣa*;[72] he has handsome cheeks or a handsome chin, *suśipra*.[73]

Though he is given a human form yet he is apprehended only by understanding, *dhiyeṣita*, and appreciated only by the wise, *viprajūta*.[74]

Like Agni, Indra too has three stations. The Vedic seers say: we invoke Indra whether he comes from this earthly region, *pārthivāt*, or from the heaven above, *divaḥ*, or from the vast firmament, *rajasaḥ*.[75]

V

We shall now take up a few other important features of the Vedic Gods. Each God has a thousand names, *sahasra-nāman*, to use an expression of the *Atharvaveda*. Indra is *puru-nāman*,[76] bearer of many names. These he also shares with other Gods. Each God has multiple functions and multiple forms, *puru-rūpa*,[77] whether he is Rudra or Agni, or Indra. These forms are spiritual and mutually shared. Mitra and Varuṇa are both sapient, *kavī*;[78] they are occupiers of spacious dwellings or are the refuge of the multitude, *uru-kṣaya*.[79] Indra, Soma and Viṣṇu are wide-striding or much praised, *urugāya*.[80] Indra and Agni move in a wide course extending over a wide space, *uru-jrayas*.[81] Varuṇa, Pūṣaṇa, Soma, Ādityas are widely praised, *uru-śansa*.[82] Indra, Varuṇa and Mitra are of powerful nature, *tuvijāta*.[83] Varuṇa and Mitra are of pure vigour, *pūtadakṣa*.[84] Indra and Varuṇa are high-spirited, *tuvi-śuṣma*;[85] Indra, Agni and Maruts are very glorious, *tuvi-*

[70] Ibid., 1.11.4
[71] Ibid., 1.10.9
[72] Ibid., 1.23.3
[73] Ibid., 1.9.3
[74] Ibid., 1.3.5
[75] Ibid., 1.6.10
[76] Ibid., 8.93.17
[77] Ibid., 2.33.9; 5.8.5; 6.47.18
[78] Ibid., 1.2.9
[79] Ibid., 1.2.9
[80] Ibid., 10.29.4; 9.62.13; 2.1.3
[81] Ibid., 8.6.27; 5.6.8
[82] Ibid., 1.24.11; 1.138.3; 8.48.4; 2.27.9
[83] Ibid., 1.131.7; 1.2.9
[84] Ibid., 1.2.7
[85] Ibid., 6.68.2

dyumna.[86] Agni, Varuṇa, Indra are all wise, *medhira*.[87] Indra, Agni and Soma are fond of invocation, *girvaṇas*.[88] Both Indra and Agni are thousand-eyed, *sahasrākṣa*;[89] both are young, *yuvā*.[90]

Each God is supreme in turn. Indra is the eldest, *jyeṣṭha*.[91] Tvaṣṭar is the earliest born, *agriyam*.[92] Even Agni, who is man's messenger to the Gods, is the supreme God in his turn. He is called the first one, *prathama*, and the chiefest Aṅgiras, *aṅgirastamaḥ*,[93] chief of those who bear the name of Aṅgiras like Sūrya, Prāṇa, Ātmā, Agni. He is called pre-eminent over the winds, *prathamo-mātariśvan*.[94]

As a result, praises and hymns that are given to one also belong to the others. "Whatever excellent praises are given to other divinities also belong to Indra, the bearer of the thunderbolt."[95] Similarly, in another Sūkta addressed to Agni, the Rishi says: "Whatever we offer in repeated and plentiful oblation to any other deity is assuredly offered to thee."[96]

---

[86] Ibid., 1.9.6; 3.16.3; 5.87.7
[87] Ibid., 1.31.2; 1.25.20; 6.42.3
[88] Ibid., 1.5.7; 1.45.2; 9.64.14
[89] Ibid., 1.23.3; 1.79.12
[90] Ibid., 1.11.4; 1.12.6
[91] Ibid., 1.100.4
[92] I bid., 1.13.10
[93] Ibid., 1.31.2
[94] Ibid., 1.31.3
[95] Ibid., 1.7.7
[96] Ibid., 1.26.6

CHAPTER 11

Vedic Gods: One God: Many Gods: Advaita

This way of looking at the Godhead is disconcerting to the Western schematic mind. In the Vedic approach, there is no single God. This is bad enough. But the Hindus do not have even a supreme God, a führer-God who presides over a multiplicity of Gods. If there has to be a plurality of Gods, as is the case in all polytheistic religions, there could at least be a tabulated statement of Gods arranged in some order of superiority and inferiority, each God having some distinctive characteristics of his or her own. But here we have no such thing, no ranking, no order of seniority and precedence, no hierarchy, no recognizable magistracy; it is all anarchy. This melee could not even be called a pantheon—a body of Gods, however disordered (Gk. *pan+theos*); it is a body of demons and evil spirits, a pandemonium (*pan+daimon*).

It seems that the Hindus were either confused about their Gods or that these Gods were not jealous enough to be like the God of the Bible. The Hindus worshipped their Gods in turn with the same supreme epithets. It seems to be like a philanderer wooing several women at the same time with the same vows, promises, and protestations and telling each in turn that she is the only beautiful and true one for him. If they only knew what the man was doing, there would be trouble enough for him! In like manner, if a Hindu God knew what his worshipper was telling his rival God, it would either expose the devotee's insincerity or the powerlessness of his God!

But there is another approach, quite a different one, which was adopted by the people of the Vedas. According to this approach, "Reality is one but the wise call it by different names; they call him Indra, Mitra, Varuṇa, Agni, Yama, Mātariśvan."[1] Reality is like the Ganges; different villages along its banks are differently named but they are all on the same river; the people drink the same water and their soil is watered and fertilized by the same source. The Reality is like an ocean rolling against different continents; you taste it anywhere, it is the same. The Reality is like a nugget of gold; it is the same at the corners, at the top, or at the bottom or in the middle. Like a lump of sugar, it is sweet at all points. Similarly, whether you go East or West, South or North, you move in the same pervading space and you meet the same truth and principle of things.

The Hindus do not call their Gods either 'One' or 'Many'. According to them, what they worship is One Reality, *ekam sat*, which is differently named. This Reality is everywhere, in everything, in every being. It is One and Many at the same time and it also transcends them both. Everything is an expression, a play, an image, an echo of this Reality.

In Vedic literature, the question of the number of Gods was no point of dispute and agitated no mind. The number could be increased or decreased at will. It all depended on the principle of classification, on the context, and on the viewpoint. In *Bṛhadāraṇyaka Upaniṣad*, to a repeated question regarding the number of Gods, Yājñavalkya's answer is first three thousand three hundred and six Gods, then thirty three, then three, then two, then one and a half, then one.[2] But this 'one' God of Yājñavalkya was not that of Christian or Muslim theology. For on further questioning, this one God turned out to be "Breath", *Prāṇa*, also called "Brahma, the Yon (*tyat*)."[3] Yājñavalkya was speaking the language of the Yoga, the language of the *sādhanā* of the *Prāṇa*, the spiritual churning of the life-force.

II

There are two ways of regarding the Godhead. In one approach, God is a jealous one. He brooks no other. He is Ishmael-like, his

---

[1] *Ṛgveda*, 1.164.46 [2] *Bṛhadāraṇyaka Upaniṣad*, 3.9.1 [3] Ibid., 3.9.9

hand against everyone and everyone's hand against him. But in the Vedic concept, all Gods are friends, one and equal. Brahmaṇaspati is associated with Indra, Soma and Dakshiṇā; they are invoked jointly.[4] The Maruts are requested to come along accompanied, *saṃjagmano*, by Indra, and both are called of "equal splendour", *samāna varcasā*.[5] Indra and Varuṇa are offered "conjoint praise", *sadhaṣtutī*.[6] They are invoked together. "I invoke you both", says the worshipper;[7] or, "come Agni with the Maruts", is the reputed prayer of the devotee in another hymn.[8]

They offer sacrifices to "Indra, Vāyu, Bṛhaspati, Mitra, Agni, Pūṣaṇa, Bhaga, the Ādityas and the Maruts".[9] They solicit "Mitra and Varuṇa and Ṛtu" to be present at their sacrifice.[10]

Western scholars have called the above approach "henotheistic". Henotheism is a compound of two Greek words and it means "towards one God". It is supposed to be a progress from the polytheism of primitive tribes and a groping towards the perfection of Semitic monotheism. The *Shorter Oxford English Dictionary* defines it thus: The belief in a single god without asserting that he is the only God: a stage of belief between polytheism and monotheism. *Webster's Seventh New Collegiate Dictionary* defines it as "the worship of one god without denying the existence of other gods".

The Hindus need not accept this description of their approach. For, as we have seen, their approach is neither polytheistic, nor henotheistic, nor monotheistic, but advaitic. They worship One Reality, neither many Gods nor One God. But if henotheism also means, as the English dictionaries tell us, a belief in a God without saying that other Gods are false or that that God alone is true, then this word does describe something of the temper of the Vedic and Hindu religion.

This approach to Gods has bred a spirit of religious tolerance and freedom. Ancient Rome, Greece and Egypt—all polytheistic

[4] *Ṛgveda*, 1.18.5
[5] Ibid., 1.6.7
[6] Ibid., 1.17.9
[7] Ibid., 1.17.7
[8] Ibid., 1.19.1-9
[9] Ibid., 1.14
[10] Ibid., 1.15.6

cultures—were relatively free from religious wars though they had their full quota of wars otherwise. Rome, Alexandria and Athens were open places where different religions met and discussed freely. When St. Paul visited Athens, he was invited by the Athenians to speak about his doctrines. He did avail himself of the opportunity but it is obvious that he did not feel at home in this atmosphere of free enquiry. For the compilers of the New Testament say that "the Athenians and strangers which were there spent their time in nothing else, but either to tell, or to hear some new thing".[11]

St. Paul represented not the Spirit's impatience with what is only cerebral but a passionate attachment to a fixed idea which is closed to wider viewpoints and larger truths of life.

In polytheistic Rome too, men of different religious persuasions and sects met and built their temples and worshipped in their own way. But this freedom disappeared when Christianity, the religion of One True God, took over.

Monotheism was not always a spiritual idea. In many cases, it was an ideology. It was consolidated in wars and in turn it led to further wars. There were wars between different tribes, each tribe claiming its own God to be supreme. Eventually, the Gods of the tribe that lost in battle were supplanted by Gods of the winning side. Or, sometimes, a tribe exchanged its Gods for power. It accepted the Gods of the conquered people in order to consolidate its power over them. Or, perhaps, there was a larger association to create, an empire to consolidate, or other nations and tribes to conquer, and the idea of a 'One True God' was handy in the pursuit of this object. Thus, diplomacy, the sword, systematic vandalism, all played their part in making a particular god supreme. From very early days, the One God of Christianity was bound up with the imperial needs of Rome. In more recent times, the Biblical God has tried to consolidate what the European arms and trade have conquered.

---

[11]Acts, 17.21

III

But monotheism is not altogether without a spiritual motive. The Spirit is a unity. It also worships nothing less than the Supreme. Monotheism expresses, though inadequately, this intuition of man for unity and for the Supreme.

There is also the fact that once polytheism is admitted, there is a tendency for Gods to multiply to inconveniently large and unmanageable numbers. It is easy to get lost in their crowd. The soul hungers for something simpler and more definite and more manageable. On such occasions, religious reformers appear and use a big broom and sweep away the plethora of Gods. What remains is perhaps not deep enough from a certain angle; but the mind is certainly less cluttered and it can breathe more freely.

When the urge for unity is spiritual, the theology of One God is no bar and the seeker reaches a position no different from *Advaita*, from *ekam sat*. He realizes that *God alone is*, and not that there is only One God.

But if the motive for unity is merely intellectual, it helps little, spiritually speaking. God remains an outward being and does not become the truth of the Spirit. It does not even help to reduce the number of Gods; instead it multiplies the number of Devils—if Christianity is any guide in the matter. We know how Medieval Christianity was chock-full of them. In fact, they occupied the centre of attention of the Church for many centuries to the exclusion of everything else. During these centuries, it was difficult to say whether the Church worshipped God or these devils. One authority calculated that the number of demons was six and a half million. According to another authority, there were 79,05,926 lesser demons presided over by 72 Princes of Hell. All of them were intriguing against the Church and were undermining its work and authority. Each of the Princes had his allotted work. Lucifer promoted pride, Asmodeus lechery, Belphegor sloth, and so on.

The Church also abounded in Gods though they were not as

plentiful as the devils. But these were not recognized as such because they appeared in the guise of angels, cherubims, and seraphims. They were organized in nine orders all battling with opposing demons in helping the Church in the task of saving the souls of her flock.

IV

Like monotheism, polytheism too is subject to the despiritualizing influences of the externalizing mind. The Gods of polytheism tend to lose their inwardness and thus they also lose their inner unity. In India, this has happened again and again. On such occasions, sages appeared and by their life and work tried to restore to the Gods their inwardness and unity. The Upanishads were one such attempt. In the *Kenopaniṣad*, it is shown how Agni, Vāyu, Indra exulted in the victory won for them by Brahma. But they soon learnt their lessons. Agni with what he thought was his own power could not burn a straw, nor Vāyu carry it off. Thus they discovered that their strength was not their own, and that their victory did not belong to them.

Again, like monotheism, polytheism too has its spiritual motive. If monotheism represents man's intuition for unity, polytheism represents his urge for differentiation. Spiritual life is one but it is vast and rich in expression. The human mind also conceives it differently. If the human mind was uniform, without different depths, heights and levels of subtlety; or if all men had the same mind, the same psyche, the same imagination, the same needs; in short, if all men were the same, then perhaps One God would do. But a man's mind is not a fixed quantity and men and their powers and needs are different. So only some form of polytheism alone can do justice to this variety and richness.

Besides this variety of human needs and human minds, the spiritual reality itself is so vast, immense, and inscrutable that man's reason fails and his imagination and fancy stagger in its presence. Therefore, this reality cannot be indicated by one name or formula or description. It has to be expressed in glimpses from many angles. No single idea or system of ideas could convey it adequately. This too points to the need for some form of polytheism.

A pure monotheistic God, unrelieved by polytheistic elements, tends to become lifeless and abstract. A purely monotheistic unity fails to represent the living unity of the Spirit and expresses merely the intellect's love of the uniform and the general. Similarly, purely polytheistic Gods without any principle of unity amongst them lose their inner coherence. They fall apart and serve no spiritual purpose.

The Vedic approach is probably the best. It gives unity without sacrificing diversity. In fact, it gives a deeper unity and a deeper diversity beyond the power of ordinary monotheism and polytheism. It is one with the yogic or the mystic approach.

These ideas could be expressed in another way. Monotheism is not saved by polytheism, nor polytheism by monotheism, but both are saved by going deep into the life of the soul. In the soul, there are no distinctions between the One and the Many. God or Gods do not exist there in the same way as they exist in the intellect. Depending on the cultures in which they are born, mystics have given monotheistic as well as polytheistic renderings and interpretations of their inner life and experiences. Both of these renderings have been noble and edifying. But One God or Many Gods, purely on the intellectual plane, feed no soul.

V

In this deeper approach, the distinction is not between a true One God and the false Many Gods; it is between a true way of worship and a false way of worship. Wherever there is sincerity, truth, and self-giving in worship, that worship goes to the true altar by whatever name we may designate it and in whatever way we may conceive it. But if it is not desireless, if it has ego, falsehood, conceit, and deceit in it then it is unavailing though it may be offered to the most True God, theologically speaking. "He who offers to me with devotion a leaf, a flower, a fruit, or water, that I accept from that striving devotee", says Lord Krishna in the *Gītā*.[12]

He also assures us that "those who worship other Gods with faith worship me", for "I am the enjoyer of all sacrifices".[13] Devotion, faith, austerity, striving in the soul—they all belong to Him; they are His food; they can never go to a false God though so declared by a rival theology.

The fact is that the problem of One or Many Gods is born of a theological mind, not of a mystic consciousness. In the *Atharvaveda*, the sage Vena says that he "sees That in that secret station of the heart in which the manifoldness of the world becomes one-form", *yatra viśvam bhavatyekarūpam*;[14] or, as in the *Yajurveda*, "where the world is rested in one truth", *eka nīḍam*.[15] But in another station of man, where not his soul but his mind rules, there is opposition between the One and the Many, between God and Matter, between God and Gods. On the other hand, when the soul awakens, Gods are born in its depths which proclaim and glorify one another.

Gods are bound to appear when the spiritual consciousness awakens; though in another sense they also fall away, God as well as Gods, with all their outward, anthropomorphic forms, and along with all our conceptions of them, however sublime and exalted.

Yes, even God falls away. For there is a spiritual consciousness which can do without God. Buddhism, Jainism, Sāṃkhya, Taoism and Zen confirm the truth of this observation. In fact, in Buddhism and Jainism, though Gods are plentiful, there is very little of One

---

[12]*Bhagvadgītā*, 9.26

[13]येऽप्यन्यदेवताभक्ता यजन्ते श्रद्धयान्विताः। तेऽपि मामेव कौन्तेय यजन्त्यविधिपूर्वकम्॥
अहं हि सर्वयज्ञानां भोक्ता च प्रभुरेव च।
— *Bhagvadgītā*, 9.23-24

A different attitude is expressed in the following declaration: "He that is not with me is against me." — *New Testament*, *Matthew*, 12.20

[14]वेनस्तत् पश्यत् परमं गुहा यद् यत्र विश्वं भवत्येकरूपम्।
— *Atharvaveda*, 2.1.1

[15]वेनस्तत् पश्यन्निहितं गुहा सद्यत्र विश्वं भवत्येकनीडम्।
— *Yajurveda*, 32.8

God. Yet in spiritual perception, insight and attainment, these religions are not less than those where One God rules the roost and is the sole cock of the walk. Spengler tells us, though on the conceptual rather than the spiritual plane, that there are equally profound religions and religious convictions that are theistic, pantheistic, polytheistic and even atheistic.

In any case, those in whom spiritual consciousness has awakened, God is "not this that people worship here", *nedam yadidam upāste*,[16] neither One God nor Many Gods, but something different, something more inward, and transcendental.

Worship is in man's soul and the divine glory is reflected in everything and in every symbol. Therefore, the Vedic seers worshipped Him in many Forms and under many Names. "Veneration to the great Gods, veneration to the lesser, veneration to the young, veneration to the old, we worship all the Gods as well as we are able,"[17] that is their attitude. A true heart's homage cannot go waste; it cannot go to false Gods; in a divine economy, it is taken up by That which is the secret meaning and the principle of truth in everything.

VI

This discussion should help to promote our understanding not only of Vedic religion and Vedic Gods but also of a whole archetypal spiritual consciousness which expresses itself in the language of Many Gods; and as a result should also help us to understand better the old religions of Europe and Asia which are no more; it should also help us to see in a new light the old Gods of Egypt, Persia, Greece, Rome, the Gods of the Scandinavian and Baltic countries, the Gods of the Germanic, Celtic, and Slavic peoples. The beliefs of the best of these people were probably not polytheistic but, in deeper interpretation, advaitic.

---

[16] *Kenopaniṣad*, 1.5-8

[17] नमो महद्भ्यो नमो अर्भकेभ्यो नमो युवभ्यो नम आशिनेभ्यः ।
यजाम देवान् यदि शक्नवाम मा ज्यायसः शंसमा वृक्षि देवाः ॥
— *Ṛgveda*, 1.27.13

In the cultural history of the world, the replacement of Many Gods by One God was accompanied by a good deal of conflict, vandalism, bigotry, persecution and crusading. These conflicts were very much like the 'wars of liberation' of today, hot and cold, openly aggressive or cunningly subversive. Success in such wars played no mean role in making a local deity, say Allah of certain Arab tribes, win a wider status and assume a larger, monarchical role.

Looking at the whole thing from the perspective of today, it is difficult to say whether the replacement was enriching or impoverishing in the spiritual and cultural sense. In most cases like these, outer symbols change without making any significant changes in their psychic meanings. It would, therefore, be difficult to hold that the present Gods of Semitic origin are superior to the now defunct Pagan Gods. There was a time when the old Pagan Gods were pretty fulfilling and they inspired the best of men and women to acts of greatness, love, nobility, sacrifice, and heroism. It is, therefore, a good thing to turn to them in thought and pay them our homage. We know pilgrimage, as ordinarily understood, as wayfaring to visit a shrine or a holy place. But there can also be pilgrimage in time and we can journey back and make our offerings of the heart to those Names and Forms and Forces which once incarnated and expressed man's higher life. They are holy Names and Symbols.

Here, in the preceding pages, we could do no more than discuss the broader principles of spiritual life, the wider perspective from which Gods could be viewed, illustrating what we had to say with the help of Gods in the Vedic pantheon with which we have greater familiarity and rapport. But there is no doubt that the same principles hold good for Gods of other nations and other times too. We believe that if we could look at those Gods in the light of this discussion, they too could become meaningful to us and we could enter into their larger spirit and be filled with them.

But any approach to a specific pantheon of a specific country or people will still require entering into a special ethos and even imbibing a special mentality. If this could be done, thus recapturing the understanding of the old Gods, there is no doubt that it could vivify the cultural history of the nations believing in those Gods. The present generations of many countries tend to regard their past as a benighted period of their history. A more understanding approach towards their Gods of old will work for a less severe judgement about their past and their ancestors. It will also fill the generation gap, not the one we talk about the most these days but a still wider one, the general rootlessness of a whole nation. Gods provide an invisible link between the past and the present of a nation; when they go, the link also snaps. The peoples of Egypt, Persia, Greece, Germany and the Scandinavian countries are no less ancient than the peoples of India; but they lost their Gods, and therefore they lost their sense of historical continuity and identity.

Today, there is a spirit of revolt amongst Western youths against their parents' religion. Some are seeking light in new symbols. One of the most fruitful channels for them could be to explore the symbols of their more remote forefathers. This could help to broaden and deepen the religion of their parents with the religion of their ancestors.

What is true of Europe is also true of Africa and South America. The countries of these continents have recently gained political freedom of a sort, but it has done little to help them and to give them a spiritual identity. If they wish to rise in a deeper sense, they must recover their soul, their Gods, their roots in their own psyche; there has to be a spiritual reassertion, a resurrection of their Gods. If they need any change, and there is no doubt they do, it must come from within themselves as a part of their own experience. If they do enough self-churning, then their own Gods will put forth new meanings in response to their new needs. They have to make the best of their own psychic and spiritual gifts and discover their own Gods within themselves. No people can import their Gods ready-made and rise spiritually under the aegis of imported deities, saviours and prophets.

But one cannot retain old Gods or revive their memory artificially. One should develop a spiritual way of looking at things.

One should live with these Gods and spend much time with them. In a sense, all Gods are jealous Gods. They want a person wholly with themselves before they become wholly his. One has to dwell with them and meditate on them before they become vivifying forces. If there is sufficient aspiration, invoking, and soliciting, there is no doubt that even Gods apparently lost could come back again. They are there all the time. For nothing that has any truth in it can be destroyed. It merely goes out of manifestation; but it could reappear under propitious circumstances. So could the old Gods come to life again in response to new summons. Where are the minstrels and priests who could preside over the birth of these Gods?

And yet the birth of Many Gods will not herald the death of One God; on the other hand, it will enrich and deepen our understanding of both. For One God and Many Gods are spiritually one. It is only on the conceptual plane that they are opposed.

This point needs stressing. For in the past, the controversy between One God and Many Gods or between My True God and Your False God led to many rolling heads and much spilled blood; and, even today, there is no dearth of hotheads and the discussion still tends to polemics, bad blood, and frayed tempers. There are still organized churches and missions out to make war on the false Gods of the heathens. We are afraid that even the present discussion will be regarded with less than a friendly eye by the theologians of One God. But to them we say that we have no disrespect for their point of view and we mean no hurt to their feelings. At the present time, when most theologies, whether pluralistic or monotheistic, are suspect and have lost their appeal, we should be able to approach the problem in a more chastened mood and in a more understanding way.

CHAPTER 12

Names of Gods: Post-Vedic

In the last chapter, we saw that Gods are neither polytheistic nor monotheistic, but both are expressions which try to convey the truths of a higher consciousness. We also saw that the Names of Gods are, at heart, the truths of man's own higher life.

We now turn to the post-Vedic Gods and their Names. This will make our discussion more comprehensive and also help towards deeper self-discovery.

The Vedic conception of Godhead was not primitive, nor was it an aberration. On the contrary, it represented a fundamental movement and sensibility of the psyche; therefore, it had a shaping influence and it set the pattern for all subsequent developments in the conceptualization of Gods. True, as we might expect, during the long passage of time, there have been many changes in the idiom and even in the mentality of the people. Some of the old Gods have been forgotten; others have become less important and yet others are remembered under different names. But behind all these changes, one can still observe a continuity in the spirit of approach.

Some old Gods like Sūrya and Agni are not exactly forgotten but others have come up so fast that they have pushed the former into the background; but they still continue to be sufficiently important. Sūrya has no longer temples dedicated to him as he did a thousand years ago but he is still invoked daily by millions of people through the *Gāyatrī mantra*. Agni has lost his pre-eminent position but even today, in millions of homes, he is worshipped daily with grains of rice and the first cake is offered unto the fire as oblation. Millions of people when they first light a lamp every evening, or even put on the electric light, salute it. To them, the spirit of the Sun descends into the lamp for the night; many others pay homage to the light of the lamp as a symbol of their chosen deity who, of course, differs from people to people and region to region.

The new Gods also share the characteristics of their Vedic predecessors. They too are plural in form but unitary in essence. Like the old Gods, they are also psychic or physical in origin, the physical soon turning into the psychic and the psychic taking on a physical garb. Each of these new Gods also has multiple Names which are at heart the truths of man's own being and which are revealed only to people of purity and meditation.

Even today when the modes of worship have considerably changed, the Names of Gods remain very important. The best of hymns and the great music built on them are nothing but Gods' Names, other devotional ideas and sentiments merely hanging on them. According to the Yoga of Devotion, certain Names like Aum, Rāma, Kṛṣṇa, Śiva are as big as the whole Reality. These names encompass all the worlds and all the levels of existence. Their vibrations, sounds and meaning enter into all sounds and meanings and words.

Every God has a thousand Names whether he is Viṣṇu or Śiva or Gaṇeśa, Rāma or Kṛṣṇa or whether she is Gaṅgā (the Ganges), Gāyatrī or Sītā or the Mother Goddess in her various manifestations as Kālī or Durgā or Sarasvatī. The *Mahābhārata* gives 1,008 Names for Śiva,[1] 1,000 for Viṣṇu,[2] 108 Names for the Sun.[3] But while all Gods have these Names, we shall choose by way of illustration only four deities and give their more important Names to show how they interpenetrate each other and how they embody man's psychic truths and meanings. This should help in deepening our study of man and his Gods and his higher life.

Of these four deities, two, Viṣṇu and Śiva, are psychic in origin; but the other two, Sūrya and Gaṅgā, have also physical co-

---

[1]*Mahābhārata*, Anuśāsanaparva, 17, 31-153.

[2]Ibid., 149, 14-20.

[3]Ibid., Vanaparva, 3, 16-28.

ordinates. Of the last two, Sūrya has a peculiar universality. He is non-Aryan, Aryan, Vedic, and post-Vedic. He was worshipped also by the Red Indians, the Incas and the Mexicans, who all developed their religious cultures independently, insulated from any influence originating in the old world. He is a visible God, *pratyakṣa devatā* (also one of the Names of Gaṅgā), *par excellence*.

Let us see what a Hindu worships in these symbols and Gods. When we study the Names of these different Gods, we find that each God is possessed of the highest attributes, and these are the same attributes. This makes it clear that the Hindus worship the same deity in all these symbols. This is not only an observable fact of experience, it also makes logical and spiritual sense. Whatever symbol the soul chooses, it seeks to worship through it, its highest image of perfection, light and truth. It is its natural aspiration; it will not be satisfied with anything less than this image. So whatever be the deity chosen for worship, it will invest him or her with all the attributes of perfection, light and power.[4]

In these names we see that each God is supreme and each has the attributes of the supreme. He is the creator of the world as well its supporting principle; therefore, the names of all the elements are His Names. He is beyond time but He is also the measure of all times; therefore, the names of the *yugas*, the months and days are His Names. He is the object of all knowledge; He is also the means

---

[4]Every nation had these symbols in so far as they represented the best in that nation's soul. For example, the Norse had beautiful names for God. One such name was 'Balder', meaning the 'bright one'. Another name was 'Heimdallr', meaning the 'world-gleam', or 'he who shrines over the world'. What beautiful names! Light and illumination were necessary attributes of a deity and all nations and races had names of God or Gods which brought out this attribute prominently.

The Scandinavians used the term 'Tivar' for their Gods, which means the 'shining ones', and is related to the Sanskrit *devas*, which means the same thing. Other attributes too were not neglected. God Frey is 'battle-bold'. Balder is a youth, attractive and graceful. Goddess Sif has luxuriant golden hair. Odin is grey-haired and yet has none of the weakness of age. Thor is also conceived as being in the prime of life.

by which we know Him. So, in a way, all names are His Names. All names proclaim Him, manifest Him. He is beyond every name and yet all names derive from Him.

II

If we look at the Names of the four deities we have chosen for discussion, we are struck by certain features. For example, we find that each God is also the other.

Śiva is Viṣṇu, Kṛṣṇa, Keśava, Hṛṣikeśa, Hari—all popular names for Viṣṇu. Śiva is also Ravi and Bhānu, names for Sūrya.

One of Viṣṇu's names is Śiva. Viṣṇu is also Āditya, Sūrya and Savitā.

Sūrya is Viṣṇu, Rudra, Skanda, Varuṇa, Brahmā, Indra, Yama, Soma, Śiva.

Gaṅgā is Vaiṣṇavī, Kamalā, Indirā, Kālī, Girisutā or Pārvatī (consort of Śiva), Durgā, Brāhmī (power of Brahmā), and Lakṣmī (consort of Viṣṇu).

Each has the attributes of the supreme Godhead.

Śiva is Aja (Beginningless), Ananta (without End), Amara (Immortal), Amita (Boundless), Amogha (Unfailing), Aśoka (beyond Grief).

Viṣṇu is Aja (Beginningless), Ananta (Endless), Atula (Peerless), Acyuta (Steadfast), Vītabhaya (beyond Fear), Pūrṇa (All), Pavitra (Holy), Aśoka (beyond Grief), Viśoka (without Grief), Acala (Unmovable), Aprameya (Immeasurable), Amṛta (Deathless), Ameyātmā (One whose Being cannot be Fathomed), Avyaya (Imperishable), Abhū (Unborn), Puṇya (Virtuous), Anādi (without Beginning), Anāmaya (Free from Disease), Ādhāra (the Ground; the Base), Adhātā (One who is without a Creator).

Gaṅgā too is Viśokā (without Grief), Aśokā (beyond Grief), Atulā (Incomparable), Amoghā (Unfailing), Acyutā (Steadfast), Ādhārā (the Base), Ānandā (Bliss), Apārā (having nothing Beyond), Abhayā (Fearless), Amṛtā (Deathless), Pūtā (Purified), Puṇyā (Virtuous), Pūrti (Fulfilment).

Surya is Aja (Beginningless), Ananta (Endless).

Each one is also the first and the highest one, and also the most esteemed.

Śiva is Ādi (the Prime Source), Devadeva (Lord of Gods), Pitā (Father), Mātā (Mother), Pūrṇa (All).

Viṣṇu is Purātana (Ancient), Sanātana (Eternal), Prabhu (Lord), Deveśa (God of Gods).

Gaṅgā is Mātā (Mother), Īśvarī (All-Powerful), Jyeṣṭhā (the Eldest), Praṇavākṣararūpiṇī (consisting of the Syllable Om), Ādyā (the first One), Muni-Stutā (praised by Sages).

Sūrya is Ādideva (the First God), Devadeva (Lord of Gods), Sanātana (the Eldest), Mātā (Mother), Pitā (Father), Sarvādi (One Before All), Sarvalokanamaskṛta (worshipped by All).

Each combines all the opposites.

Śiva is Sat-Asat (Being: Non-being), Kṣara-Akṣara (Perishable: Imperishable), Eka-Naikarūpa (One: Multiform), or Naikātmā (of manifold nature).

Similarly, Viṣṇu is Sat-Asat (Being: Non-being), Eka-Naika (One: Many), Amūrti-Anekamūrti (having no Form: having many Forms), Sūkṣma-Sthūla (Intangible: Tangible).

Sūrya is Jīvana-Mṛtyu (Life: Death), Sraṣṭā-Saṃvartaka (Creator: Destroyer), Vykta-Avyakta (Manifest: Unmanifest).

Each is also the source, the embodiment and the secret Self or truth of everything.

Śiva is Sarva (All), Bhava (Being, Source), Bhūtālaya (Ground of all Beings), Bhutāśraya (Refuge of all Beings), Sarvātmā (the Self of All), Sarvabhūtātmā (Self of all Beings).

Viṣṇu is Prabhava (Source), Bhūtabhāvana (Creator of Beings), Bhūtabhṛt (Nourisher of Beings), Bhāva (Reality), Bhartā (Nourisher), Bhāvana (Creator), Bhūtātmā (the Self of all Creatures), Pūtātmā (the Pure Self), Paramātmā (the Highest Self), Dharmātmā (the Virtuous Self).

Sūrya is Bhūtāśraya (the Refuge of all Beings), Bhūtapati (the Lord of Beings), Carācarātmā (the Self of all that Moves or is Still), Sūkṣmātmā (the Subtle Self), Praśāntātmā (the Tranquil Self), Viśvātmā (the Self of the World).

Gaṅgā is Bhāvā (Creator), Jagadyoni (Source of the World), Jagadātmā (Self of the World), Paramātmasvarūpā (Form of the Highest Self).

Each is also the Gods and the Elements of Nature.

Śiva is Anila (Wind), Anala (Fire), Ākāśa (Sky), Soma (Moon), Bhānu (Sun), Savitā (Sun), Vāyu (Wind), Vāta (Breeze).

Viṣṇu is Anila (Wind), Ravi (Sun), Anala (Fire), Pavana (Wind), Vahni (Fire).

Sūrya is Sāgara (Sea), Jīmūta (Cloud), Aindhanāgni (Fuel-fire), Āpa (Water), Teja (Fire), Pṛthivi (Earth), Kha (Ether), Ākāśa (Sky), Vahni (Fire), Jaṭharāgni (Digestive Fire).

Each is beyond time, yet it gives names to all the planets and all the measures of time.

Śiva is Kṣaṇa (Moment), Kāla (Time), Candra (Moon), Sūrya (Sun), Śani (Saturn), Ketu (Ketu), Kṣapā (Night), Ṛtu (Season), Māsa (Month), Pakṣa (Fortnight), Kali (Kaliyuga).

Sūrya is Kṣapā (Night), Yāma (A period of 3 hours), Kṣaṇa (Moment), Saṃvatsara-kara (Cause of the Year), Kṛta (Satya-yuga), Tretā (Tretā-yuga), Dvāpara (Dvāpara-yuga), Kali (Kali-yuga), Soma (Moon), Aṅgāraka (Mars), Budha (Mercury), Bṛhaspati (Jupiter), Śukra (Venus), Śanaiścara (Saturn).

Each one is full of valour, vigour and beauty.

Śiva is Ajita (Unconquered), Vijaya (Victory), Tejopahārī (He who takes away all the strength and dignity of an opponent by a mere glance), Maheṣvāsa (Great Archer), Dhanvī (Archer), Bāṇahasta (Wielder of Arrows), Ūrdhvareta (Living in Chastity),

Ūrdhvaliṅga (the Chaste One), Mahākarma (Doer of Great Deeds), Manovega (travelling with the Speed of the Mind), Vikramin (Valorous), Sthāṇu (Steadfast), Sthira (Immovable), Sumahāsvana (making a Great Sonorous Sound), Vidāruṇa (Terrible); He is Sahasra-bāhu (having a Thousand Arms), Sahasra-pāda (having a Thousand Feet), Sahasra-mūrdha, (having a Thousand Heads), Mahāmūrdhan (having a Great Head), Mahā-netra (having Great Eyes), Mahā-hanu (having a Great Jaw), Mahā-grīva (having a Great Neck), Mahā-kambu (having a Stark Neck), Mahoraska or Mahāvakṣas (Broad-chested), Mahā-danta (having large Teeth), Mahājihva (Long-tongued), Hiraṇya-bāhu (Golden-Armed), Śubhākṣa (Auspicious-Eyed), Bahumāla (Multi-Garlanded), Mahāmāla (wearing a Great Garland).

Similarly, Viṣṇu is Ugra (Impetuous), Jetā (Victor), Jaya (Victory), Durjaya (Unconquered), Vīra (Valiant), Kṣama (Capable), Duratikrama (Unsurpassable), Vijaya (Victory), Īśvara (Lord), Dhanvī (Archer), Sudhanvā (Skilful Archer), Maheṣvāsa (Great Archer), Sthira (Immovable), Sthāṇu (Steadfast), Sthavira (Stable), Dāruṇa (Terrible), Bhīma (Great), Vasuretas (of Plentiful Energy), Sughoṣa (Sonorous), Suvarṇaretas (of Golden Vitality), Sarvaga (Going Everywhere), Ūrdhvaga (Going High). He is Sahasra-mūrdha (having a Thousand Heads), Sahasra-pāda (having a Thousand Feet), Sahasrākṣa (Thousand-Eyed), Viśva-bāhu (having Arms on every side), Śatānana (Thousand-Faced), Mahākṣa (Great-Eyed), Vīra-bāhu (with Powerful Arms), Mahā-krama (Moving Greatly), Viśva-mūrti (having the world for his Form), Mahā-mūrti (Great-bodied), Dīptamūrti (of Splendid Form), Śatamūrti (having a Hundred Forms), Suvarṇavarṇa (Golden Complexioned), Hemāṅga (Golden Limbed), Varāṅga (having Wonderful Limbs), Sundara (Beautiful), Sulocana (with Beautiful Eyes), Candanāṅgadin (wearing Sandalwood Bracelets).

Gaṅgā is Jayā (Victory), Vijayā (Victory), Īśvarī (Ruler), Krāntalokatrayā (encompassing the Three Worlds). She is Taporūpā (the Embodiment of Austerity), Tapomayī (Full of Austerity), Prasannarūpā (of Joyous Form), Putā (Pure), Prītā (the Happy One), Abhirāmā (Pleasing), Rāmā (Beautiful), Kānti

(Splendour), Tejogarbhā (Source of Vitality), Ānandā (Blissful), Adbhutarūpā (of Wonderful Beauty), Āścarya-mūrti (of Wonderful Form), Kamalākṣī (Lotus-Eyed), Ghoṣā (Sonorous), Sundarī (Beautiful).

Sūrya is Jaya (Victory), Viśāla (the Vast), Dīptāṃśu (of Blazing Rays), Śauri (Heroic), Śuci (Pure), Śīghraga (of Quick Move-ment), Arvindākṣa (Lotus-Eyed).

They have also other qualities of knowledge, light, askesis, joy, and truthful resolve.

Śiva is Sarvajña (All-Knowing), Satya-vrata (of True Resolve), Kānta (Resplendent), Soma (Moon-like), Sompā (Drinker of the Soma juice), Śānta (Tranquil), Kṣama (Forbearing).

Viṣṇu is Śuci (Pure), Satyadharma (of true Law), Su-vrata (of right Resolve), Saha (Forbearing), Kṣama (Forgiving), Śrīnivāsa (Abode of Beauty) Mahātapa (the Great Ascetic), Sutapa (Rightly Austere).

Gaṅgā is Vrata-rūpā (Embodiment of Resolve), Puṇyagarbhā (Source of Righteousness), Śāntā (Tranquil), Somā (Moon-like), Puṇyā (Righteous), Premasampannā (full of Love), Punānā (Purifying), Dhṛti (constant in Resolution), Dharmadhurā (the Highest Dharma or the Nave round which Dharma revolves), Śraddhā (Faith), Srīmatī (full of Grace and Beauty), Dharma-jalā (whose Waters are Dharma), Nityotsavā (always Festive).

Sūrya is Maitreya (Friend), Karuṇānvita (endowed with Compassion).

Each is everywhere.

Śiva is Sarvatomukha (facing All), Sarvadvāra (the Universal Gate), Sarvadhātu (Essence of All).

Viṣṇu is also Sarvatomukha (Facing All).

Sūrya is Viśvatomukha (facing All Sides), Sarvatomukha (facing All), Sarva-dhātu (Essence of All).

Gaṅgā too is Viśvatomukhī (facing All), Visvā (All-pervading).

Each is also the great goal, the wide gate, the way and the knowledge that leads to the destination.

Śiva is Nirvāṇa (the Great Ceasing-to-be), Śānti (the Great Peace), Puruṣa (the Spirit), Sākṣī (Witness), Kṣetrajña (Knower). He is Mokṣadvāra (the Gate of Liberation), Svarga-dvāra (the Gate of Heaven), Prajā-dvāra (the Gate to all Beings). He is also the knowledge that leads to this goal. He is Yoga (Yoga), Yogī (Perfect in Yoga), Yama (Self-Control), Niyama (Vows), Dama (Restraint), Śama (Renunciation), Guru (Teacher), Mantra (the Creative Word).

Viṣṇu is Śūnya (the Great Void), Śānti (the Great Peace), Brahma (the Highest Knowledge), Nirvāṇa (Ceasing to-be). He is also the Mārga (the Path), Stuti (Hymn of Praise), Yoga (Yoga), Yogī (Perfect in Yogas), Sadā-Yogī (Established in Yoga), Yogīśa (the Lord of Yogins), Mahā-yajña (the Great Sacrifice), Veda (the Vedas), Vedāṅga (limbs of Vedic knowledge), Vedavit (Knower of the Vedas).

Gaṅgā is Nirvāṇajananī (Mother of Nirvāṇa), Yoginī (Perfect in Yoga), Yogayoni (Source of Yoga), Dharmdhurā (the Acme of Righteousness), Ṛksvarūpā (one whose Soul is the *Ṛgveda*), Vedavatī (of the Form of the Vedas), Mahā-vidyā (the Highest knowledge of Brahma).

Sūrya is Mokṣadvāra (the Gate to Liberation), Svarga-dvāra (the Gate of Heaven), Yogin (Perfect in Yoga), Vedakartā (Creator of the Vedas), Vedavāhana (Vehicle of the Vedas).

Each is a great teacher, protector and saviour.

Śiva is Gati (Resort), Parā-gati (the Supreme Resort), Bhaktānam Paramā-gati (the Supreme Resort of Devotees), Brahmaloka (the World of Brahma), Parama-Brahma (the Supreme Brahma). He is also the Mantra (the Secret Word), Parama-Mantra (the Ultimate Secret Word), Yoga (Union), Guru (Teacher), Yajña (Sacrifice), Tīrtha Deva (the Luminous Pilgrimage).

Viṣṇu is Niṣṭhā (Perfection), Parāyaṇam (the Last Resort), Śaraṇam (Shelter), Dhāma (Abode), Gati (Refuge), Gati-Sattama (the Most Excellent Refuge), Muktānām Paramāgati (the Refuge of the Liberated Ones), Satām-gati (the Refuge of Good Men), Sad-Gati (the True Refuge), Āśrama (the Rest), Sannivāsa (the True Dwelling). He is also Yoga (Union or Path to God-Union), Yama (Self-Restraint), Niyama (Vows), Guru (Teacher), Mantra (the Secret Word), Mārga (the Way), Yajña (the Sacrifice), Mahā Yajña (the Great Sacrifice), Jagataḥ Setuḥ (the Bridge by which to cross over to the other Shores of the World).

They are also the great healers and bearers of all gifts to their worshippers. Therefore, they are loved.

Śiva is Vara (Boon), Varada (Giver of Boons), Kāma (Desire), Goptā (Protector). He is Jīvana (Life), Dhanvantari (the Great Physician), Tāraḥ (the Great Boatman, through whom one crosses the Ocean of Existence), Iṣṭa (Beloved).

Viṣṇu is Jīvana (Life), Prāṇa (Breath), Tāraṇa (the safe Passage). He is Sukhada (Giver of Happiness), Goptā (Protector), Pāpanāśana (Destroyer of Sin), Kāma (Desire), Kāmahā (Destroyer of Desires), Pāvana (Purifier), Varada (Giver of Boons), Maṅgalam-param (the Highest Well-Being), Iṣṭa (Beloved).

Gaṅgā is Jīvana (Life), Mahauṣadha (the Great Medicine), Prāṇa (Life), Prāṇadā (the Giver of Life), Ārogyadā (the Giver of Health), Dīrghāyukāriṇī (the Giver of Long Life), Tarī (Boat), Tārā (one who takes you across the World of Existence). She is Nityasukhadā (the Giver of Eternal Happiness), Kalyāṇī (Promoter of Well-being), Varapradā (Boon-Giver), Puṇya-pradā (Giver of Righteousness), Dhanadā (Giver of Wealth), Dharmakāmārthamokṣadā (Promoter of the Four Aims of Life—Dharma, Kāma, Artha, Mokṣa), Pāvanī (Purifier), Yajñaphala-pradā (Giver of the Fruits of Sacrifice), Yogasiddhi-pradā (Giver of the Perfections of Yoga), Yogajñānapradā (Giver of the knowledge of Yoga), Yuktibuddhidā (Giver of Reason and Intelligence), Yaśodā (Giver of Fame), Iṣṭā (Beloved).

Sūrya is also Jīvana (Life), Dhanvantari (the Great Physician), Kāmada (He who fulfills desires), Varada (Giver of Boons), Prāṇadhāraka (Life-Support).

All are equally worshipful.

Śiva is Īḍya (Worthy of Worship), Śaraṇya (Shelter), Vareṇya (Worthy), Pāda (Goal).

Viṣṇu is Mahejya (Worthy of Great Offerings), Mānya (Esteemed), Stavya (Worthy of Praise), Mahārha (Greatly Worthy).

Gaṅgā is Kāmyā (to be Desired), Vandyā (Worthy of Salutations), Mānyā (Esteemed), Namyā (Worthy of Homage), Yajanīyā (Worthy of Sacrifice), Ejyā (Worthy of Oblations), Īḍyā (Worthy of Worship), Namaskāryā (Venerable), Vedyā (to be Known), Dhyeyā (to be Meditated upon), Cintyā (Worthy of Reflection), Japyā (Worthy of Chant), Dhanyā (Worthy of Thanksgiving), Yācyā (Worthy of Being Wooed).

All have their seats in the secret cave of the heart and are difficult to realize.

Śiva is Guhāvāsī (dwelling in the Secret Cave of the Heart).

Viṣṇu is Durlabha (difficult to Attain), Durgama (difficult to Reach), Guhya (Inscrutable), Gabhīra (Deep), Gahana (Mysterious), Gupta (Secret), Dur-Dhara (One difficult to Hold).

Gaṅgā is Gūḍharūpā (Enigmatic), Guhāvidyā (Secret Science), Durgamā (One difficult to Reach), Durāsadā (One difficult to Approach), Durlabhā (difficult to Attain).

On the other hand all of them are said to be easily attainable.

Gaṅgā is Dhyānagamyasvarupā (One who is reached through Meditation), Dharmalabhyā (attainable through Dharma), Bhaktasulabhā (Easily attained by Devotees),

Viṣṇu is Sulabha (easily Attained).
Śiva is Prakāśa (Manifest), Suvijñeya (easily Known), Prasāda (easily Pleased), Abhigamya (Within Reach).

They are also the Great Questions, the Key to all Answers, the Great Exposition of everything.
Śiva and Viṣṇu are Kim (Who? What? The Great Question to be pondered over), Yat (the Self-Proved, the Self-Evident), Tat (that which brings out, enlarges upon, the Great Exposition).

CHAPTER 13

Names of Gods: Their Attributes

In the preceding chapter, we have been treading on holy ground —at least, that is what one felt. One can easily see how the Names of Gods find a ready response in one's own psyche; which shows how in some way they incarnate the truths of one's own mind and heart. Through the Names of Gods we deal with the truths of our own being, truths deep, mighty, lofty, sublime. Gods live in the soul and, therefore, their truths are the soul's own truths, of the soul at its most divine.

But there is a sense in which the Gods are *outsiders*. They are external to the ordinary desire-consciousness which we best know and with which we are most familiar. They live in the region unreached by our ordinary interests, experience, and meanings. Therefore, the truths conveyed by the Names of Gods ring a bell only in those minds which have an intuitive feeling for the sublime. To others, these Names are no more than a catalogue of unreal and high-sounding words.

The Names we have given above are only samples. The *Mahābhārata* says that Śiva has ten thousand Names out of which it gives only one thousand and eight. In fact, when the mind opens spiritually, all names become Names of Gods. A God is *viśvanāman*, to use an expression of the *Atharvaveda*. In that sense, all lists of Names are incomplete—they cannot be otherwise. But while everything is completed and made good in due course on the spiritual path, and in some way every Name also expresses the God-life wholly and indivisibly, even a partial list has its importance and purpose. It tells us, though only intellectually, something about the spiritual Reality. It tells us, for example, about its unity, its comprehensiveness, its immanence, its transcendence; it tells us about the mutuality of Gods; it tells us how the opposites are united in the Spirit; it tells us how Gods remain unknown in some important sense.

II

One obvious thing that the list tells us is that the Deity that is worshipped under different Names is the same. Sometimes it is called Śiva, sometimes Viṣṇu, sometimes Gaṅgā, sometimes Sūrya. But all these Gods are the same in essence; they are the Names of the same Name or Deity.

But to call this Deity 'One' will not do. For it is also 'Many'. In fact, this is the only way by which something of the power, majesty, variety, ubiquity, universality, and glory of the divine and the riches of the spiritual life can be suggested. How could the vast Reality of the Spirit be grasped and expressed by one Name? This Reality casts Its shadow differently and our mind also conceives It differently. The Intellect, the Sky, the Sun, the Moon, Fire—all are different shadows of the same Reality. They have to have different names even when they are not different. Even an ordinary thing like water has many names in its different forms as ocean, river, cloud, steam, snow, sap, etc. Then why not the Reality of the Spirit which is much more subtle and fundamental, which is the substance of everything that we see, which is in the seer as well as in the seen and the seeing?

In the way the Hindus conceptualize the higher life, the Gods do not stand apart. They are not autonomous. They are part of each other. Each God is supreme but each is also the other. And understandably so. For each expresses the same Reality. Each is fashioned from the same substance—like a pitcher, a pot, a plate, a saucer, a jug fashioned from the same earth.

In his *Lights On The Vedas*, T.V. Kapali Sastry quotes Yāska to show that the Vedic Gods are characterized by mutuality of birth and nature, *itaretara-janmānaḥ* and *itaretara-prakṛtayaḥ*. Not only that, but it could equally be said that they also share the same names, *itaretara-saṃjñakāḥ*, or *itaretara-nāmānaḥ*; they also signify one another, *itaretarārthāḥ*; they are also the form and soul of each other, *itaretara-svarūpiṇaḥ* and *itaretarātmānaḥ*. This is so because they are fashioned from the same substance, *abhinna-sattvāḥ*, and represent the same principle, *ekatattvāḥ*.

The post-Vedic Gods follow this lead and are conceived after the Vedic pattern.

III

The lists of the Names of Gods reveal another great characteristic, their deep inner unity. There is unity not only between one God and another but also between the Names of the same God. For example, some of the Names for Śiva are *Nirvāṇa*, *Śānti*, *Yoga*, *Yama*, *Niyama*, *Dama*, *Śama*. And very justly so. For how can there be *Nirvāṇa* without *Yoga*; and how is any *Yoga* possible without *Yama*, *Niyama*, *Dama and Śama*? The unity is written all over the Names. That which destroys desire also destroys anger, destroys sorrow, brings fulfillment, brings blessings and happiness, takes away fears and makes life pure and meritorious. That is why some of the Names of Viṣṇu are *Kāmahā*, *Krodhahā*, *Śokanāśana*, *Puryitā*, *Śrīkara*, *Sukhada*, *Bhayāpaha*, *Pavitra* and *Puṇya*.

IV

These Names are also comprehensive. They signify not only a God's amiability and goodness but also his other attributes, his power, majesty, glory, authority, dexterity, skill, strength and even his more awesome and terrible aspects. The Old Testament says: "With God is terrible majesty." But a latter-day pious and sentimental spirituality fought shy of developing this aspect of God. It thought that God was all love, syrup, goodness and agreeableness—as conceived by the human mind. But Hindu spirituality developed and gave Names and Forms to all the divinely mysterious forces of life, to all that was operative in the human psyche, destructive and terrible or constructive and agreeable. Therefore, the Deity is not only *Śiva* and *Jīvana*, Auspicious and Life; It is also *Mṛtyu*, *Śarva* and *Rudra*, or Death, Slaughter and Terrible. In the *Gītā*, Shri Krishna, the very embodiment of beauty and attractiveness, also shows his "strange, awesome and terrible form", *adbhutaṃ rūpam ugram*, "at which the three worlds are terror-stricken", *lokatrayam pravyathitam.*[1] In Hindu iconography, one often finds images of Kālī in her more destructive and terrible aspects. This has put off, through misunderstanding, some Western scholars, and has provided an opportunity for others to malign the Hindu religion.

V

Another conclusion that can be drawn from the lists of the Names of Gods is that the Godhead exists fully and indivisibly in each Name and Symbol. The Sun, the Sky, Fire, the Moon—they all incarnate that Truth, and that Truth lives in each of them wholly and indivisibly. It means that each is a perfect symbol of worship and what is given by one symbol is also given by the other.

And yet if one single symbol tries to set itself up as the one sole symbol, it loses its integrality. In the *Bṛhadāraṇyaka Upaniṣad*, this point is well brought out in a dialogue between Dṛptabālāki Gārgya and Ajātaśatru of Kāśi. Each time the Person in the Sun or in the Moon, or in the Lightning, or Space or Wind, is worshipped as the sole symbol of the Brahma, the symbol is found insufficient. By pretending to be sole, it becomes partial and, therefore, also yields partial knowledge and partial power. "Brahma is not known by this much knowledge only, *naitāvatā viditam bhavtīti.*"[2]

But the lists of Names also yield another conclusion which is just the opposite of the above. God lives in each Name and Symbol equally, wholly and indivisibly; yet He also transcends all Names and all Symbols. The *Gītā* says; "By me, all this universe has been extended in the ineffable mystery of my being; all existences are situated in Me, not I in them. And yet all existences are not situated in Me; behold My divine Yoga; Myself is that

[1]*Bhagvadgītā*, 11.20

[2]*Bṛhadārāṇyaka Upaniṣad*, 2.1.14

which supports all beings and constitutes their existence but does not dwell in them."[3]

VI

This stresses God's transcendence and his essential unknowability. In spite of man's visions, experiences, yoga and *samādhi*, there is a sense in which God remains unknown. In fact, the more one knows Him, the more the mystery clings to Him. There is also a knowledge of God which consists not in saying what He is but in saying what He is not. There is a mystery and a riddle at the heart of the Godhead which can never be fathomed. The unknowability or rather the *negated* knowledge of God, *asamprajñāna*, is a fundamental insight of the mystic tradition.

Therefore, when St. Paul saw in Athens an altar with the inscription, "To The Unknown God",[4] he could have interpreted it spiritually. But he chose a lesser way. To him the inscription only proved that the Athenians were "superstitious".[5] Then he proceeded to say, "Whom therefore ye ignorantly worship, him declare I unto you."[6] Then he began to proclaim to them what God is and how he has created the world and called upon them to repent and told them about the Day of Judgement, the Resurrection and the Mediator.

In Hindu thinking, the Unknown does not become known that easily. God does not reside in debates which the Greeks loved and St. Paul disliked; but nor does He reside in a preacher's harangues and declamations. Some of the Names of Gods are *Durlabha* (difficult to attain), and *Durgama* (difficult to reach). He is *Guhya* (secret), and *Gabhīra* (deep). But He can be known through

---

[3]मया ततमिदं सर्वं जगदव्यक्तमूर्तिना। मत्स्थानि सर्वभूतानि न चाहं तेष्ववस्थितः॥
न च मत्स्थानि भूतानि पश्य मे योगमैश्वरम्। भूतभृन्न च भूतस्थो ममात्मा भूतभावनः॥

— *Ḅhagvadgīta*, 9, 4-5

[4]Acts, 17.23

[5]Ibid., 17.22

[6]Ibid., 17.24. We have quoted from the "King James Version" of the Bible; but the more recent "Revised Standard Version" gives a different rendering which is less objectionable.

Yoga, through meditation, through purity and sacrifice. He is *Dhyānagamyasvarūpa* (who can be reached through meditation), *Dharmalabhya* (attainable through Dharma), and *Jñānagamya* (attained by gnosis).

VII

God has two natures: transcendent and immanent. Corresponding to them, there are two methods of *sādhanā*, spiritual practice. One is the well-known method of *neti neti*, Not this, Not this. This method is based on the fact that God's nature is transcendental. He goes beyond every symbol, name, form, conception, or image. It is the worship of the unknown in the known; it is the 'unknown God'.

The other is the method of *etadvaitad*, This also is That. Through this method, one finds God residing wholly and indivisibly in each symbol. The world is a theophany.

Gods' Names bring out clearly the two natures of the Godhead. God transcends every one of His Names; He also lives fully and indivisibly in each of them. In one Name, we must be able to see all the Names; in one God, we must be able to see all the Gods; otherwise, our knowledge of a God and His Names is not sufficient. We must also be able to see that a God exceeds all his Forms and Names, individually and collectively. The heart of a God is an enigma.

CHAPTER 14

Names of Gods: Their Transforming Power

We now come to another attribute of the Names of Gods—their shaping and transforming power. To emphasize its importance, we are taking it up separately. But since it introduces rather a new dimension which goes beyond the scope of this book, we shall do no more than give it a cursory look. As a result, this chapter which could be the longest would be the shortest.

The discussion of the Names of Gods is not a mere theoretical exercise in theology; it is intimately concerned with the higher meanings of life and is, therefore, deeply human. It has also an eminently practical side. Gods' Names are meant for meditation; and through meditation for assumption and assimilation of something of their higher meanings and powers. If one meditates on these Names, they not only reveal their deeper meanings but they also tend to shape one in their image.

We have already seen how meditation on the Name of Krishna reveals its higher, psychic meanings and also reveals its other related Names; but if the aspiration is sufficiently pure and the meditation sufficiently sustained, a process of change sets up within us and we begin to grow into the likeness of the higher meanings of those Names. In fact, we cannot know the higher meanings without in some measure *becoming* those meanings. As we begin to make acquaintance with them, we also begin to appropriate them, assimilate them; and in turn we are assimilated by them. The Name is revelatory, appropriatory, assimilatory and transformatory.

II

This change, this transmutation, this alchemy is a necessary part of all mystic quest. Man does not merely seek an interpretation of the world; he seeks a change in his being. He is made in the image of God and he keeps seeking this image; he keeps trying to become more God-like.

This likeness to God, *theotupia* as the Greeks called it, is best effected by meditating on one of the Names or Forms or Powers of God. According to the Upanishads, men tend to become what they worship, invoke, aspire to, dwell with and meditate upon. By meditating on the different Names and Forms of Gods, we receive something of their vibrations and grow in their likeness.

In the *Bṛhadāraṇyaka Upaniṣad*, this point is well brought out. There, Ajātśatru tells us that he who worships the Person in the yonder Sun as Pre-eminent, as the head and king of all beings, himself becomes pre-eminent and becomes the head and king of all beings; he who worships Him in Lightning as the Brilliant one becomes brilliant; he who worships Him in Wind as the Conqueror becomes a conqueror; he who worships Him in Fire as the Vanquisher himself becomes a vanquisher; he who worships Him as Life (*asu*) lives his full span of life; and he who worships Him as the Shining One outshines all and so on.[1]

Thus by meditating on Gods's Name *Pūta*, purity, we ourselves become pure; by meditating on His Name *Vidyā*, knowledge, we acquire knowledge. In this way, an aspirant is made in the image of God and His different Names. Each Name of Gods is a mine, a treasure. It holds within it a whole universe. Through invocation, aspiration, meditation, devotion, works, sacrifice and purity, one can take out of it as much as one can. Each Name is also a veritable mantra; when meditated upon, it becomes a power, the creative Word, the saving Word.

III

If man knew how to invoke Gods' Names properly, they could raise him up individually and would also have important social bearing. For example, some of the Names of Gaṅgā are *Amalā*, *Vimalā*, *Nirmalā*, meanings Spotless, Stainless, Pure. If we had

[1]*Bṛhadāraṇyaka Upaniṣad*, 2.2-13

meditated on these Names, we could not have polluted this great river, nor, in fact, any other river, with such a clear conscience; we could not have made it into a receptacle for all kinds of waste and turned it into an open sewer.

Similarly, if we had meditated on the different elements of nature, the sky, the air, the water, the earth, they would have revealed many of their secret Names. Among these Names would have been *Śuci*, *Śuddha*, *Svaccha*, *Adūṣita*, *Pavitra*, *Puṇya* or the Radiant, the Bright, the Clear, the Undefiled, the Pure, the Auspicious.

If we had meditated on these Names and they had left their vibrations within us, if we had seen something of their beauty and purity, if we knew that they are part of us and we are part of them, then how could we pollute our atmosphere, shut out the sky with smog, choke the air and the earth with poisons of all kinds? If we knew that the Earth was a Mother, we could not have mined away its soil and exploited and depleted it with such unscrupulousness. If we had meditated on Compassion, *Dayā* or *Anukampā*, we could not have made a roaring business out of the pain and tears of our fellow-creatures, the animals and the birds. The world suffers from exploitation, cruelty, bestiality, and pollution because the Gods and their Names have gone out of our lives, because we have forgotten the secret by which we could invoke the power and knowledge that reside in those Names; therefore, they no longer yield their deeper meanings, nor exercise their formative and transforming influence. The Gods have withdrawn; but they could be invoked again by the power of aspiration, askesis and meditation.

Glossary of Sanskrit Terms

adharma, the wrong, the false
ādhibhautika, the material, the physical
ādhidaivika, the supernatural, the divine
ādhyātmika, the Spiritual
agriyam, the earliest born
ahaṃkāra, individuation, the Ego Principle
ahiṃsā, non-violence
ananta, endless
anatḥkaraṇa, internal organs of cognition
anudātta, grave sound in Vedic pronunciation
anukampā, compassion
aparigraha, non-possession, non-covetousness
artha, object to which a *śabda* (sound) refers
aśabda, silent
asaṃprajñāna, negated Knowledge
asteya, non-stealing
avibhāga, indivisible
avyakta, Primordial Reality, potential

bhāva, mood
bhūmi, level or status of consciousness
brahmacarya, celibacy, chastity
buddhi, Intelligence, Intellect

cakṣu-āyatana, the world of seeing

dama, self-restraint
dayā, compassion
deha, the body, the Physical Principle
dhāma, resting place, station
dharma, the right, the true
dhāraṇā, continued meditation
dhyāna, reflection, meditation
dhyāna-bhūmi, the contemplative plane of consciousness
dyotitārtha, with no sound but only meaning

ekāgra, ingathered, concentrated
ekāgra-bhūmi, state of one-pointedness
ekam sat, the One Reality
eka nīḍam, rested in one truth
eka rūpam, merged in one form
etadvaitad, This also is That

gīrvaṇas, fond of invocation
grahaṇa, the inner perception
grāhya, the object
gṛhtṛ, the observer

guhāhitam, concealed in the cave of the heart

indriya, the senses

jagannidānam, Cause of the World
jyeṣṭha, the eldest

kāma, desire
kāma-bhūmi, the sensuous plane of consciousness
karma, the law of action, potentiality
karuṇā, compassion
kavi, sapient, sage
kāyāgni, body-fire, nerve-force
kīrtana, singing Gods' names
kramarūpa, sequence and form

madhyamā-vāk, status of speech where it becomes mental
mahat, Vast, Intelligence
manas, mind
mantra, sacred or secret word
medhira, all-wise
mūla-prakṛti, the Primordial Principle
mūlādhāra, the solar plexus

nābhi, the navel
nāma, the subject, thought
nāma apīcyam, the secret name
nāma-rūpa, Subject and Object, thoughts and things
nāmāni guhya, the secret names
neti-neti, not this, not this
niravayava, without any vocal limbs or outer expression
nirvāṇa, extinction, liberation
nitya, permanent

parā-vāk, status of speech where it is established in its own luminous form
paśyanti-vāk, status of speech where there is no distinction between the denoter and the denoted
pluta, protracted vowels
prakṛti, the Primordial Reality
prāṇa, the Vital Principle
prāṇā-kośa, the Vital Sheath
prathama, the first one
pratigha, confrontation
pratyakṣa devatā, visible God
puru-nāman, bearer of many names
puru-rūpa, of multiple functions and forms
pūta-dakṣa, of pure vigour

rajas, quality of restlessness, passion
rājasika, restless, passionate
Ṛk, a Vedic verse
rūpa, the object, the things

śabda, sound
śabda-niṣpatti, origin of sound
sādhanā, spiritual practice
sahasrākṣa, thousand-eyed
sahasra-nāman, thousand-named
śama, tranquility
samādhi, absorption
sāmaga, singer of the *Sāmaveda*
sāmāpatti, advanced stage of meditation in Buddhist Yoga

saṃskāra, mental tendency
samyaka ājīvikā, right livelihood
samyaka vyāyāma, right exertion
saṃjñā, consciousness
śānti, peace
sarvataḥ saṃhṛta-krama, concentrated
satnāma, the true or secret name
sattva, the quality of purity, true nature
sāttvika, pure, clear
satya, truth
śauca, purity
sparśa, contact
śravaṇa, listening to scriptures or Gods' Names
śrutigocara, heard by the inner ear
sūkta, a Vedic hymn
svadhyāya, study of scriptures, self-reflection
svarita, circumflex sound in Vedic pronunciation
svarūpajyotiḥ, established in its own luminous form

tamas, the quality of intertia, dullness, obscurity
tāmasika, inert, dull, obscure
tuvi-dyumna, very glorious
tuvi-jāta, of powerful nature
tuvi-suṣma, high spirited

udātta, acute sound in Vedic pronunciation
uru-gāya, wide striding, much praised
uru-jrayas, moving in a wide course
uru-kṣaya, occupiers of spacious dwellings, the refuge of the multitude
uru-śaṃsa, widely praised

vaikharī-vāk, the spoken word, the word produced in the mouth
vāk, speech
varṇātiritkta, beyond the syllables
vastusārūpyam, that which takes the form of the thing it stands for
vedanā, sensation, feeling
vijñāna, the Intellect
viśvanāman, including all names

yantra, mystical diagram
yuvā, youthful

Index